Of
Scottish
Ways

By Eve Begley

DILLON PRESS, INC.
MINNEAPOLIS, MINNESOTA

Dillon Press, Inc., 500 South Third Street
Minneapolis, Minnesota 55415

Printed in the United States of America

Library of Congress Cataloging in Publication Data

Begley, Eve.
 Of Scottish ways.

 (Heritage books)
 SUMMARY: Examines the traditions, history, government,
religion, and other aspects of Scottish life.
 1. Scotland. [1. Scotland—History. 2. Scotland—Social life
and customs] I. Title.
 DA757.5.B43   941.1   76-46439
 ISBN 0-87518-122-8

CONTENTS

*For Roy,
my favorite Sassenach*

SCOTLAND

SHETLAND ISLANDS

FAIR ISLE

ORKNEY ISLANDS

THURSO

LEWIS

HARRIS

N. UIST

BENBECULA

S. UIST

BARRA

SKYE

GREAT GLEN

INVERNESS

ABERDEEN

FORT WILLIAM

MULL

OBAN

DUNDEE

PERTH

STIRLING

EDINBURGH

GLASGOW

BERWICK

ISLAY

ARRAN

GALASHIELS

CAMPBELTOWN

AYR

DUMFRIES

CHEVIOT HILLS

Two "ga' in' bodies" talk with a kilted Scot by historic Eilean Donan Castle.

Chapter 1

SCOTLAND TODAY

IF YOU WERE ASKED to describe Scotland to someone from the jungles of the Amazon, you might say,

"Scotland is a small country surrounded on three sides by water and joined on its southern border to a larger, more densely populated place called England."

The climate in the geography books is optimistically described as temperate—a word anyone who has lived there would argue with. A great deal of rain falls all year round, and summers, like the one in Shakespeare's sonnet, have a short lease.

The average temperature in summer is around sixty-four degrees and in winter forty-four degrees, although it can rise as high as the humid eighties on occasion and fall below freezing in winter. Snow falls but rarely lies long, save on very high ground.

The people who live in Scotland are a sturdy race, short to medium in stature in the Lowlands, medium to tall in the Highlands. Many of them have red or sandy hair and are fair-skinned. The dialects are many, but the chief language is English. Gaelic is also spoken in the west and northwest.

There are about one hundred and seventy Scots per square mile on the average (although that shrinks to a mere seven in some outlying districts), compared with nine hundred English per square mile farther south. The Scots are, in spite of all rumors to the contrary, of a friendly and hospitable nature—even verging on the generous in many cases.

The country is divided into three distinct geographic areas known as the Highlands, the Central Lowlands, and the Southern Uplands. The Southern Uplands contain the border area between Scotland and England, which is known as the Borders. Two-thirds of the five and a quarter million people live in the highly industrialized Central Lowland belt. The country's chief natural resources are coal, iron, and oil —although small quantities of lead, zinc, and talc are also present.

There are 186 inhabited islands—with underwater electric cables feeding power to most of them. There are snow-capped peaks for skiing, mountain torrents and rivers for fishing, sea and inland lochs for sailing, and rolling hills for walking—all within an area of 33,000 square miles lying in approximately the same latitude as southern Alaska and Sweden. Days are short in winter, but in summer you may play tennis until ten o'clock at night.

The highest mountain in all the British Isles is Ben Nevis, located in the western part of Scotland. It is 4406 feet high and always has a snowy "tablecloth" on top. (The Cameron Clan have a legend that their chieftain, Lochiel, will always hold his lands as long as that tablecloth remains there.)

There are thirty-three counties, named as follows:

Aberdeen	Bute	Fife
Angus	Caithness	Inverness
Argyll	Clackmannan	Kincardine
Ayr	Dumfries	Kinross
Banff	Dunbarton	Kirkcudbright
Berwick	East Lothian	Lanark

Midlothian	Perth	Stirling
Moray	Renfrew	Sutherland
Nairn	Ross & Cromarty	West Lothian
Orkney	Roxburgh	Wigtown
Peebles	Selkirk	Zetland (or Shetland)

Today most of the Scottish people are engaged in professional and scientific services, construction, engineering and electronics, transportation, and miscellaneous public jobs—a breadth of activity which sounds like that of many other modern countries.

Occupations which used to play a more important role in the economy but have suffered a decline are textile manufacturing, mining, shipbuilding, and fishing. The coalfields of Fife, Lanark, Ayrshire, and Stirlingshire used to be much busier than they are now—in fact, many have been closed down. And the shipyards of the River Clyde, which for a long time turned out the most efficient ocean liners in the world, have been in a partial slump for several years. For decades the word "Clyde-built" meant perfection, but some of the old ways have vanished with the old days.

On the east coast, the busy port of Dundee once did a brisk business trading in jute with India, but that too has declined. At the same time Dundee became a popular home center for jams, jellies, and marmalades, which it continues to produce.

The capital city of Edinburgh, often called "the Paris of the north," is a beautiful city with a gracious main street flanked by gardens and elegant buildings, surmounted by its famous grey stone castle. It is a city of lawyers and printers, scholars and tourists.

Glasgow, Scotland's largest city, with more than one and a quarter million people, has many industries and is an active financial center. It is a city of engineers and business people; its residents are friendly and warm and its ancient cathedral stark and dignified.

Several new towns, like Glenrothes, East Kilbride, and Cumbernauld (which was redesigned on the site of a very old village), have appeared in Scotland since World War II. They have helped meet an urgent need for housing in the country.

Agriculture still plays an important, though increasingly mechanized, part in the lifestyle of the Scots. They grow barley, wheat, oats, and sugar beets and produce excellent beef cattle, of which the Aberdeen Angus is the best known. They are also doing advanced research in pig breeding at stations like Cornton near Bridge of Allan.

The fishing industry, which for generations provided Scotland's staple diet of fresh herring, still does an impressive job, and most Scots include fish regularly in their weekly menus. It's not too long since fishwives wearing striped aprons and caps and carrying creels of fresh fish on their backs stepped off buses in inland towns to bring fish from the markets of Aberdeen and Arbroath to ready home buyers. Now refrigerated trucks ("lorries") bring the fish fast to the fish shops, and the traveling fishwives are a thing of the past.

Back in 1943 a parliamentary act established a new industry in the Highlands—H.E.P. (Hydro Electric Power). With offshoot industries started since then, about fifteen thousand people are now employed in this field. A nuclear reactor at Dounreay up on the farthest north coast has made jobs for many, and now the oil industry is doing the same for Aberdeen and the surrounding area.

Yes, Aberdeen, a gracious city of sparkling granite up on Scotland's northeast coast, has become the new oil boom town of the decade.

Up until a few years ago if you asked Aberdonians about

the possibilities of their city becoming an oil town, they would have looked at you in disbelief and said, "Fit are ye talkin' aboot, man? We've naethin' here but fish an' whisky."

Today Aberdeen still has fish and whisky. It is the third largest fishing port in Britain, with 120-odd trawlers bringing in a hundred thousand tons of fish a year. And it is also one of the main whisky distilling areas in Scotland. But since 1970, when the first major oil discovery was made in the British sector of the North Sea (as designated by the 1964 European Oil Treaty), Aberdeen has become a boom town.

Pipe-laying barges, production platforms, and deep water drill sites—all have become part of the new Aberdeen skyline. Special oil rigs built to withstand the one hundred-foot waves and shifting tides of the North Sea stand on giant legs around the coastline and are maintained at a cost of thirty thousand dollars per day. A new thirty-two inch oil pipeline still to be completed will be piping oil into Cruden Bay, which used to be a holiday resort. By 1980, experts predict, Aberdeen could be one of the major oil-producing areas of the world, and people are already calling the city "Europe's offshore capital."

In the meantime, millions of dollars' worth of business, in the form of new homes, dock expansion, bank and insurance company investments, and lots of new qualified people, are changing the look of the old "Granite City." All the buildings in the center of town have had a face lift, and 30 million dollars is going into harbor improvements and 5 million to expand the fish market. Four new industrial parks have sprung up outside the town. Aberdeen is making chains, anchors, pipes, drill bits—you name it—for the oil industry, and Aberdonians are either turning it out or pulling it in through their port. There are jobs for as many Scots as want them—and for Danes, Germans, Italians, and other workers from the European continent as well.

The world's largest oil production platform, Graythorp One, now lies two hundred fifty miles out to sea off the Aberdeenshire coast. Graythorp One took twenty-five hundred people, twenty thousand tons of steel, and eighteen months to build. It is twice as high as Big Ben and weighs four times as much as the Eiffel Tower.

The enormous platform was built on its side in a dry dock especially excavated for it. When it was completed, the dock was flooded with 150 million gallons of water over a thirty-six-hour period. Then the platform was floated and carefully maneuvered through the deepest waters out to sea, a computer in the command vessel controlling every movement.

Once Graythorp One had arrived at its destination, the next task was to fill the huge tanks attached to the stern of the platform, in order to sink the platform down into three hundred fifty feet of water. As the tanks filled slowly, all hands watched with baited breath. Gradually the monstrous platform began to drop one end into the water, the other end slowly rising into the air, until at last with a great plunge the tanks settled on the sea floor and the platform was in place. Graythorp Two is under construction, and, as demand increases, more great platforms will continue to appear on the Scottish seascape.

Ask Aberdonians now about oil, and they're likely to admit it's done great things for the city. But they're also likely to add, "The oil will be fine—so long as it doesna' interfere wi' oor whisky and oor fish."

Housing is a problem not only in Aberdeen, but also in the rest of Scotland. Moving from one location to another is difficult for many. Large housing developments ("schemes") have been built by local governments since before the 1930s, and because the rents are heavily subsidized, these homes are in great demand. Young couples planning to marry may have to share their parents' homes for some time before they obtain homes of their own. Since these "council" houses are hard to get, people tend to live in them for years and years. Thus in Scotland there is little flow of labor from one area to another.

Glasgow has long been infamous for its tenements—with washing hanging out to dry and women hanging out to gossip. A window in a tenement is familiarly known as a "jaw-box," because a great deal of jawing, or gossiping, goes on from it.

In a census taken in the early 1960s, it was discovered that more Scots lived in one- and two-room houses than in all England and Wales put together—possibly because they were prepared to put up with inconvenience and slum conditions rather than pay high rents. But it is also true that rents for modern council housing in Scotland have often been lower than for equivalent accommodation in England, although in some districts wages have also been lower.

The "but and ben" (a room and kitchen) is still not unknown, but numbers are decreasing annually. Hole-in-the-wall beds (built-in beds) used to be commonly found in Glasgow tenements, and legend says they were always made long enough to fit the tall Highland policemen who moved down from the north. (But legend says a lot about Highland policemen—one favorite story being about a fellow who had to pull a dead horse all the way from Sauchiehall Street round the corner to Hope Street because he couldn't spell Sauchiehall Street for his report.)

A smaller proportion of the people own their homes in Scotland than they do in the United States, and "moving in for no down" is unheard of. If a Scots family wants to buy a house, they have to be prepared to make a large down payment, and they must also expect to deal with a fluctuating mortgage rate—terrifying thought.

The health of the Scots since 1948 has been governed by a much-maligned institution known in the United States as "socialized medicine" and in Scotland (as well as in England, Wales, and Northern Ireland) as the National Health Service.

In 1946 the British Parliament decided that everyone in Britain was eligible for a health care system which would be paid for weekly by deductions from everyone's salary. Today the British spend 5 percent of their gross national product on health care—and Americans spend 8 percent.

The average Scot contributes a certain amount each week to a service which, besides providing for a later pension, also gives access to one or more doctors in the area and provides home and hospital care, plus inexpensive prescription facilities and other services. Expectant mothers and children up to the age of five receive subsidized juice, vitamins, and milk, plus clinical and dental care. Eye care is also subsidized, and certain types of spectacle frames are available at low cost. Others may be purchased for additional cost. Dentures are available for what Americans would consider a nominal fee.

The service varies little from place to place, the only difference being that if you live in a highly congested area, you may have to wait a little longer in the doctor's office. However, the doctor will always come to the house to see you if you are very sick, and if your G.P. recommends a weekly visit from the local district nurse, you will receive that service also free of charge. Specialists are on call and will make home visits if requested to do so by the G.P.

Doctors in Scotland, like those in England, Wales, and Northern Ireland, are divided into two groups—physicians and surgeons—and you should remember to address the surgeon as "Mr.," not "Dr." The physicians run their doctors' offices outside of the hospitals, and the surgeons run the hospitals. Consequently, your family doctor may recommend surgery, but a surgeon you may never have seen before will perform the operation. Surgery is carefully regulated by active tissue committees in each hospital and there is little in the way of unnecessary operations.

Scottish medical schools have had a good name for generations, and they continue to turn out excellent doctors —many of whom, like their predecessors, settle overseas. Statistics show us that more than twenty years before the National Health Service began less than 50 percent of the doctors graduating from Scottish medical schools stayed on in Scotland to practice. It is, however, interesting to note that just a few years ago Scotland graduated approximately the same number of doctors from its population of five and a quarter million as did the state of California with a population of twenty million.

Stories in American newspapers often say there are thousands of Scots, English, and Welsh who have been waiting for months, even years, for non-emergency surgery. Certainly many Scots have elected to have their children's tonsils out or their hernias attended to in the private section of the hospital or in private nursing homes. The choice is there. But emergency situations are consistently handled immediately, and the care and cleanliness of the hospitals are of high quality, although many of the buildings are old and anything but luxurious.

An interesting facet of the National Health Service is its coverage of the thinly populated areas in the Highlands and outer islands. Special inducements attract doctors to outlying areas, and an efficient air ambulance service instituted by the National Health Service still flourishes.

When visiting Scotland, you may be struck by the healthy appearance of the children, from the rosy-cheeked babies sitting up in their prams outside the shops to the sturdy youngsters in school. The Ministry of Health claims that Britain (including Scotland) has the lowest mortality rate, for children under fourteen, in the world. You may also be struck by the behavior of these children, because many Scottish parents still believe in the old saying that children should be seen and not heard—especially when there's company around.

Altogether, Scotland today is still the kind of place people like to stay in, and it's certainly a lot easier to get around now than it was when Dr. Johnson and his friend Boswell visited it back in the late eighteenth century. (Boswell's account of their visit makes interesting reading for anyone interested in Scotland.) Like England, Scotland possesses some of the "best second class roads in the world"—a dubious compliment.

But the roads are certainly not what they used to be. Scotland too is feeling the heavy tread of modern traffic, often on roads where two cars can just pass and no more. There are modern highways in certain areas, one being the main north road, with its double-laned traffic and straight stretches. This road is far removed from the norm of winding ways that take the motorist in and out of strips of villages. The old road west from Stirling to Gargunnock and Kippen used to be one of the few straight stretches in the entire country. There you could barrel straight towards Ben Lomond rising up on the horizon.

Well into the twentieth century there were still roads being used that the Romans had laid with rectangular stone blocks known as cobbles. Most of these are now preserved in small areas for tourists to marvel at. Local people took them for granted in the same way that they accepted a thousand-year old castle or an ancient forest. Such things had always been there and were, therefore, not to be wondered at. Modern folk have become much more careful about preserving the things of yesterday, and places that used to be easily accessible even twenty years ago may now have a fence around them, an entrance fee, and a society to preserve them.

The old roads had a life of their own that has largely passed on. There were many using these roads who were commonly referred to as "ga'in' bodies"—going bodies, or people on the move.

Of all the "ga'in' bodies" of Scotland right up until the middle of this century and maybe later, by far the largest section was a group known as tinkers. Tinkers are a kind of gypsy, but the Scottish variety seem very far removed from the dark-eyed, golden-earringed gypsies of the Continent. Some are certainly dark, but many are red-headed, and a lot of women have long, chestnut-colored hair that looks as if it has been well-smoked at the campfire. The children can be scruffy and often shy; the men like to drink and play the pipes. There are some very fine pipers among the tinkers, and sometimes you can hear the strains of a lone bagpipe lilting across a moor from a tinker campsite. But they are a dying race.

Tinkers lead a life that seems quite alien to most house-dwellers. The few remaining on the roads continue the life of their ancestors, dwelling in a tent or rough leanto along a fence or a hedge. They do a little work on the farms if they can get it; they may sharpen knives or collect rags. The women may sell bits and pieces of thread and needles and elastic to the country wives. And all of them may ask at the door for "A maskin' o' tea an' a piece"—that is, a cup of tea and bread with jam. They carry their own tea-cans with them, into which the housewife puts the tea and boiling water, along with milk and sugar. In the old days before the government took over with its plans to help the poor and needy, many of the tinkers had a very irregular diet. Not that it was without merit, however. The diet was frequently expanded to include delicacies like poached rabbits and game birds, or even salmon and the odd chicken skilfully filched from a farmyard.

Most of the tinkers have left the roads. They have left their tents and moved into comfortable council houses and have put their children in regular schools where they receive steady education—instead of moving from place to place with the seasons. But there are still a few clinging with determination to the old life, refusing to be molded into the norm. Most of them live in the Highland areas, fairly far away from the rush of civilization, which is slowly encroaching on their privacy.

Scotland also has its seasonal farm labor. The fruit farms of the Carse of Gowrie increase their staffs every summer with berrypickers who may travel out by road from Glasgow and live in trailers and tents while they pick the fruit. The fruit they pick there is mostly of the soft variety—raspberries, strawberries, currants, and gooseberries. Then, in October, when the potato harvest must be gathered, many farms employ outside help, and it's not unusual to meet a group of Irish farmworkers on the road.

A sight that might seem bizarre to a visitor to Scotland would be a man on a bicycle with strings of onions tied to the crossbar. Yet it's not uncommon to see these cyclists at a certain time of year. They come over from France and are known to the locals as "Ingan Johnnies." They wear black berets, smoke Gauloises, and promote the onion trade of the Auld Alliance.

Of all the people of the roads the most lasting perhaps are the road workers themselves, who maintain the roads. Every county has its crews of laborers who keep up the surface of the roads, patching and mending where necessary. But those the Scots call "roadmen" are usually the ones in the country areas who look after the sides of the roads. They are given set stretches to care for, and it's up to them to clip and trim hedges, scythe long grasses and generally keep the roadsides in good order. It's lonely work in outlying areas, and if you meet a roadman and would like to pass the time of day with him, he'll probably be quite happy to lay aside his scythe for a while and have a friendly chat.

It is unfortunate that the number of "ga'in' bodies" has decreased so rapidly over the past twenty years—for with them Scotland has lost some of the romance of its past. Foot and bicycle have been replaced by automobile, bus, and truck, and the roads will never be quite the same again. But you may still turn a corner on a country road somewhere and find a group of tinkers crouching over a campfire, making smoky tea in their blackened billy-cans. . . .

You can also travel easily by train and steamer, as well as auto or bus, all over Scotland's thirty-three counties. And everywhere you go, you'll find green and beautiful country-side, soft air that's great for the complexion, and lots of bonnie bairns. Add to that, the kilt, the pipes, the whisky, and the odd haggis or two—and maybe you'll never want to go home again.

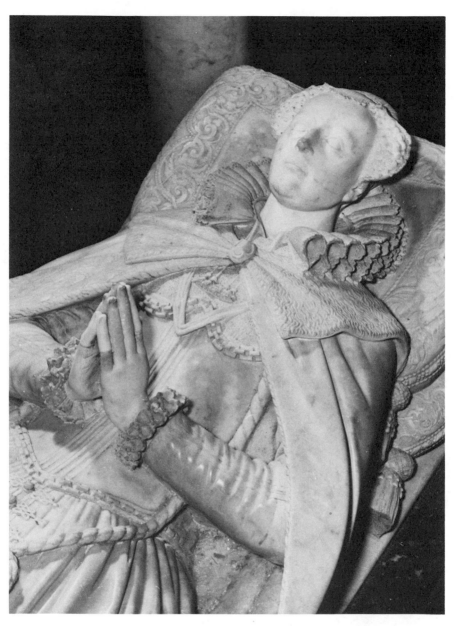

Mary, Queen of Scots, lies at rest in London's Westminster Abbey, by order of her son, James I of England.

CHAPTER 2

SCOTLAND YESTERDAY

There is nocht tua nations undir the firmament
that ar mair contrar and different fra uthers nor
is Inglishmen and Scottismen, quhoubeit that they
be within ane ile and nychtbors and of ane lan-
gage.   (—Extract from the anonymous
                          Complaynt of Scotland)

SCOTLAND'S EARLY HISTORY resembles its scenery—fascinating, but shrouded in romantic mists. Some of the first
"tourists"—the Romans—wrote letters home complaining
about the cold and the constant rain, and Tacitus wrote
poetry about "Caledonia stern and wild / Land of brown
heath and shaggy wood / Land of the mountain and the
flood."

The Roman legions never advanced very far into Scotland, being discouraged by swarms of wild men with long
hair and scanty garments who came rushing at them out of
the fog. The Romans under General Agricola did stop long
enough, however, to build a line of forts between the Forth
and Clyde rivers around A.D. 81. And they later built a wall,
named Hadrian's Wall after the Roman emperor, that be-

came a rough divider between Scotland and England. After that the Romans left the northerners pretty well alone. But they did give them a name which stuck—*Picti,* the painted ones—a name that has come down to us as the Picts. These people either painted their bodies with the blue *wode* dye (a special dye extracted from a cabbagelike plant), or tattooed themselves; no one knows for sure.

The true origin of the Picts is lost to all time. Some people believe that they were the same as the Celts or Gaels, others that they were the original ancients living there before the Celts and Gaels moved in from Continental Europe an indefinite number of years B.C. The settlers from the Continent may have regretted that move when they first experienced the Scottish climate, but they seemed to get used to it once they moved in. They were a short, dark people with long heads, who wore skins and wielded rough weapons. Some of them lived in stone towers, and we can still see a few of these "brochs" in the north mainland and islands.

When the Romans left the British Isles around A.D. 410 and rushed home to defend their empire, they left a very usable network of roads. Unfortunately for the northern natives, most of the roads were south of the border, which was another reason that the tourist trade didn't flourish in Scotland for several hundred more years. Until King George's General Wade became roadmaker-in-chief during the eighteenth century, Scottish roads were such that a rhymer said:

> Had you seen these roads before they were made,
> You would lift up your hands and bless General Wade.

And another hundred-odd years went by before a canny Scot named McAdam came up with the clever idea that tar mixed with small chunky stones made a very good covering for Scottish roads—and for roads around the world, as it happened.

After the Romans had gone, the Dalriad Irish started moving over to Scotland. In fact, it's not even fair to call the place Scotland until these Irish were well settled in, because they were indeed the *Scots,* a red- or sandy-haired people of fair skin who settled all over the southwestern area and gradually spread east and north. They mingled with the dark-haired residents and fought with the blond Vikings, who kept paying unexpected visits to the coasts. Some of the Vikings moved in permanently also, particularly around the north and northeastern shores, and there are Scots today in the Shetland Isles who might easily have been transplanted from a street in Oslo.

No one knows exactly what language these peoples spoke, but it is assumed that the Gaelic of today is a direct descendant of the early Celtic or Gaelic, and it has a definite affinity with Erse, or Irish Gaelic. The use of English crept in with the Saxons, who settled in the southeastern area of Scotland. Gradually the Gaelic tongue was confined to the north and northwest, where it survives to this day.

Around the year A.D. 560, a Christian named Columba from Ireland landed on the tiny island of Iona and earned for himself the honor of being the first bearer of the Gospel to the Scottish heathen. He established a religious order on Iona, and from that western island made determined forays into the mainland with his good news. It seems that Columba was a hard man to reject, and there are stories that make him sound as formidable as Moses. He was undoubtedly a "soldier of God" and a tough man to cross.

Actually, Saint Ninian, another evangelist, who had learned his trade in Rome, had preached Christianity to the Southern Picts, in Galloway, about sixty-five years before, but Columba is the one best remembered as the bringer of good news. Columba was not welcomed by one and all—a common thing then as now—but what he had to say was gradually accepted, and the Scots became Christians.

That didn't mean, however, that they lived happily ever after. They fought a lot, being divided into four kingdoms until the year 844, when King Kenneth McAlpin permanently united two of them, Dalriada and Pictland, making three remaining kingdoms. A mere two hundred years and lots more fighting later, the three kingdoms had become one, and Scotland became a united geographical unit. And that brought a new problem: now that the Scots were united, they decided they would like to extend their borders—a matter which kept them and the English (who didn't like the idea) busy off and on for several hundred more years.

Scotland's history now becomes very involved, with Scottish armies making forays over the border to harry English castles, and English armies headed by various irate kings stomping north to teach the rascally Scots a lesson. One of these English kings, Edward I, actually made such a habit of it that history has nicknamed him "the Hammer of the Scots."

But the Scots too had their day—and the most glorious one was Midsummer Day 1314, at Bannockburn, when the Scots army under King Robert the Bruce defeated an English army many times its size and chased the son of the Hammer of the Scots back over the border. This Scottish victory marked the way for Scotland's future, because if on that Midsummer Day the Scots had been defeated, it is doubtful whether Scotland would ever have been able to retain its independence and distinctive way of life. Without the victory at Bannockburn, Scotland might have become merely a northern adjunct to the English crown.

Scotland also discovered fairly early that it could annoy England even more by becoming an ally of France. This the Scots proceeded to do with such regularity through the famous Auld Alliance (old alliance) that the English, who were always at war with somebody, usually France, got very fed up with the whole thing. They were quite thankful when, in 1603, they could unite the crowns of Scotland and England. That way they reckoned they could keep closer tabs on their northern neighbors.

The crowns came together on the head of James VI and I (VI of Scotland and I of England); when England's Queen Elizabeth died, James was next in line to succeed to the English throne. James has the dubious distinction of having the longest legs and perhaps the worst table manners of any monarch. However, he did redeem himself in part by being an intellectual in a day when there were not too many of these around.

A century later, in 1707, the parliaments of Scotland and England were united, after a number of the Scottish members had been bribed to vote in favor of the treaty, and together Scotland and England forged ahead towards industrialization, colonization, and the foundation of the jolly old British Empire.

Going back to Scottish kings, which means kings before the union of the crowns in 1603, there's a preponderance of Jameses. And they're all Stewarts (a name derived from High Steward, or officer of the king). There are a few Roberts and Alexanders, but from 1406 until 1625, James is king (from I through VI). The Stewarts were an interesting breed. They were all intelligent, some were even intellectual, and they were all imbued with the belief that God Himself had picked them out to sit on the throne, something history books call the Divine Right of Kings.

Mary Stewart, the famous Queen of Scots, the only female exception to Jameses in 219 years, made a name for herself in world history by choosing bad friends and worse husbands and losing both her crown and her head. Mary's main problem really started at birth, because to many it seemed as if she had stronger claims to the throne of England, through her grandfather's marriage to Henry VII's daughter, than Queen Elizabeth herself, who was considered in some circles to be illegitimate. Mary, however, was a Catholic at a time when England had determined to be Protestant. John Knox, up in Scotland, wasn't too happy with a Catholic queen either, and he and Mary Stewart had many verbal battles while he was setting about the Reformation of the Scottish Church.

John Knox spent most of his time shouting out against the established church of Rome, which he and many others felt needed reform. The Protestant movement was basically opposed to the central church and the exercise of papal power over local matters. The Presbyterianism which evolved in Scotland (coming by way of Switzerland) turned out a new rule which started at the bottom. Essentially, Presbyterianism was rule by elders, or presbyters, elected by the congregation, with the minister guided by a group known collectively as the Kirk Session.

In England, the Reformation brought Episcopalianism. It maintained rule by bishops, who were not elected but appointed by an oligarchy of their peers.

Being either Catholic or Episcopalian themselves, the Stewart monarchs were always rough on the Scots Presbyterians, and the Scots were likewise determined to be awkward. John Knox, an argumentative old boy in his late fifties, reduced young Mary, Queen of Scots, to tears on several occasions. Mary's son James got so mad at his Scottish Parliament that he is said to have shouted in temper— "Nae bishop, nae king!" And when Andrew Melville, the promoter of Presbyterianism, looked him straight in the eye and told him firmly that in God's kingdom, he was "not a king, not a lord, but a *member*," James's blood pressure must have risen to a typical Stewart high.

James VI and I was succeeded by his son, Charles I, who

lost his head in 1649. He was succeeded by Oliver Cromwell, a gentleman who was unpopular with both the Scots and the Irish, not to mention many of his fellow Englishmen. Then the Stewarts came back into their own in 1660 with the restoration of Charles II to the throne, who was followed in 1685 by his brother James II. By 1688 James had been deposed for what the Protestant majority felt were dangerously Papist leanings, and thereafter followed what is known to history as the Jacobite Rebellions. The word Jacobite is derived from the Latin for James, *Jacobus,* and the James in question always was a Stewart. The first Jacobite Rebellion took place in 1715, and in 1745 the second rebellion — the more significant of the two — occurred.

James II's grandson, Prince Charles Stewart left exile in France and landed in the Highlands with a handful of friends, but within weeks he had assembled a mighty army of Highlanders. They marched on London, which they could probably have taken if they had ever agreed on anything, but they ended up being beaten ignominiously at the last battle fought on British soil, the Battle of Culloden, in 1746.

The near success of Bonnie Prince Charlie's rebellion pointed out to the government at Westminster how inadequate their internal military forces were. This caused a shuffle throughout the island—notably in the north—and since that time there have been no widespread Scottish/English conflicts, except on the floor of the House of Commons.

By the nineteenth century Sir Walter Scott's writings were fanning the fires of Scottish nationalism, and suddenly tartans, bagpipes, claymores, and heather became very popular with all Scots.

Scotland's history is as colorful as its tartans—a rich pattern of kings and queens, castles and palaces, battles and old legends. All of these are enjoyed by her visitors and cherished by the Scots at home and abroad.

Trying his skill at a sword dance during the Highland Games in Inverness-shire.

CHAPTER 3

OF CLANS, TARTANS, AND TWEEDS

THERE'S A SPECIAL MAGIC about Highland Games—the swirl of tartan, the skirl of pipes, and the suspense of competition outdoors on a hazy summer day. It's a magic that can stay with you all your life, no matter how far you may travel from Scotland.

Highland Gatherings had their beginnings in old weapon shows, when rival clans got together to show each other how skillful and well versed they were in feats of strength and self-defense. After all, if you knew the Camerons had a giant who weighed two hundred fifty pounds and could wrestle any man out of the ring, maybe you would think twice about hand-to-hand combat on Cameron land. Or if you knew the MacDouglas clan had several men who could put the shot a lot farther than your men, you might be extra wary of their ambush potential.

Today there is still rivalry among the clans, but it is more likely to be on a personal basis, one individual against another. When the Scots talk about a heavyweight champion, they may not be referring to a boxer—in Scotland a heavyweight champion is the strong man who is currently the best at throwing the hammer, putting the shot, and tossing the caber (a pine log). Usually he is a *big* man too, standing squarely on sturdy legs that know how to swing a kilt. The men competing in the Highland Games have to show how far they can throw a sixteen- or twenty-two-pound hammer and how far they can put a stone of equal weight or throw a fifty-six-pound weight up and over a bar. And they also have to toss a caber that may weigh one hundred twenty pounds and stand nineteen feet tall. To toss the caber successfully, you first balance it upright in your cupped hands, and then you run with it and throw it so that it will turn completely over—a "twelve o'clock."

Any traditional Highland Gathering will have a variety of other contests too, like dancing, running, jumping, cycling, and, of course, piping. The piping contests include individual piping and band piping, and one famous gathering in particular (the Cowal Gathering held at Dunoon every August) features a thousand pipers all piping at once—fortunately, the same tune! There can be few more heart-stirring sights to anyone with a drop of Scottish blood in his or her veins than the sight of a thousand tartan-clad pipers and drummers marching down a green hillside on waves of "Scotland the Brave."

Little girls in exaggerated Highland dress dance their legs sore on sundry platforms, hoping for rewards of silver medals. Judges have to sit through innumerable performances of the Highland Fling, Seann Truibhas, and the sword dance followed by (for some unknown reason) the Sailor's Hornpipe and the Irish Washerwoman!

Even small towns like Crieff, Blackford, and Bridge of Allan have Highland Gatherings every year—known to locals simply as the Games. The Strathallan Gathering, held the first Saturday of every August, is heralded by the arrival of "the shows" a few days before. Those are the carnival people with their roundabouts and hoop-la stalls and battered little bumper cars. They take over part of the games field and put everyone in a festive spirit ready for the big day on Saturday. You can have your fortune told, eat sticky toffee apples, and be thrilled on the swingboats there, just as you can at Coney Island—although the surrounding green hills and prim stone houses offer a little different background.

On Saturday you can sit in the grandstand with your tartan rug tucked around your knees if the day is chilly and watch six or seven different events all going on at the same time. Or you can walk around the field and watch the local people enjoying their big day of the year.

August and September are the months for Highland Games, and the Royal Family are always represented at the most famous of all, held at Braemar.

Scots abroad have taken this tradition with them, and towns all over Canada and the United States hold Highland Games every year. There's something about the Games that brings Scotland just a little nearer!

What about the clan system that first developed these Games? The word *clan* comes from the Gaelic *clann* meaning "children." So the Clan MacDonald are really the children of Donald; the Clan MacGregor, children of Gregor, and so on. The term Mac itself means "son of," the same as the Irish Gaelic form "O" in front of a name like O'Riley.

The clan system which we read about today is a fairly modern organization and dates from well after the coming of the Normans in the eleventh century. Before the clan system was established, early Celtic society was tribal in form, with different groups running their own parts of the country. The clan system was basically a feudal system, with power centered on a chieftain, who, in return for protection in time of war, took care of his people in time of peace. It was a patriarchal society and remained that way until the eighteenth century, when various factors led to its demise.

The clan chieftains were like little kings, whose rule over

their subjects was absolute. A clan saw its chieftain not as a king, however, but as a father who protected and supported them. The retinue of a chieftain always included a bard, who sang for the chieftain and was also responsible for keeping a genealogical record of the clan (for example, who got killed at which battle), personal bodyguards, a standard bearer, a harper or piper, a tatler or spokesman, and even two special men designated to carry the chieftain over running water.

Clan Donald, which includes many groups such as Keppoch, Clanranald, Sleat, and Dunyveg, to name only a few, is probably Scotland's largest clan. The clan broke up into its many parts in the fifteenth century when violent disagreements erupted over the right of succession to the Lordship of the Isles. This large northwest territory encompassed all of the west coast from Ross-shire down to the Mull of Kintyre in Argyll, as well as all the inner and outer western islands. Newly independent chieftains, who had originally been vassals of the Lordship of the Isles, now leased their land directly from the Scottish crown instead of through the Lordship. These new clans included the Macleods, Mackinnons, Mackintoshes, Macleans, and MacNeils.

Have you heard the story of the famous MacNeil who was a very proud man? Supposedly he was asked at the time of the great flood if he would like to join Noah in the ark. He refused graciously with the words, "MacNeil has a boat of his own."

A similar reorganization was taking place in other parts of Scotland at the same time. The Celtic earldoms in the eastern highlands were, like the Lordship of the Isles, disintegrating and giving way to a different system. Local chieftains, whose vassals were in part expected to take care of their own communities, replaced the old Celtic leaders, who had been hereditary chiefs of large areas. Norman families crept in with names like Fraser (from the French "fraises," denoting the strawberry leaves on their coat of arms), Rose, and de Umfraville. The old Celtic name of Clan Donnachaidh became Robertson, the sons of Robert, and the mighty Clan Diarmaid became the Campbells of Argyll. Other great clans stepping into prominence were the Camerons, led by Lochiel; the Mackenzies, led by Seaforth; and the Gordons, led by the Earl of Huntly. The most infamous Earl of Huntly is remembered in the ballad:

> Wae be tae ye, Huntly
> And whaur hae ye been?
> They hae slain the Earl o' Moray
> And laid him on the green.

In the Borders there were clans also with names like Maxwell, Graham, Elliott, Armstrong, and Johnstone. The families grew larger and more powerful and wielded as much authority as they dared within the confines of their own district—and often outside.

Although the Border clans have a rough glamour of their own, and visits to ruined keeps stir memory pictures of raids and pillaging, it is the Highland clans who have captured the world's imagination.

One of the most tragic clan stories of all time is the Massacre of Glencoe, when the MacIans of Glencoe, a branch of the MacDonald clan, were murdered one February night in 1692. William of Orange had not long been on the throne of England and Scotland, after a bitter struggle between his supporters and the supporters of the deposed Catholic king, James II. The clans who had supported James were pardoned on the understanding that they would pledge allegiance to William by January 1, 1692. Unfortunately for the MacDonalds, they were late in arriving to pledge, and

the authorities in London decided that these wild Highlanders must be brought to justice. Accordingly, a group
of soldiers who "just happened" to be Campbells made the
journey to Glencoe, and, after accepting the MacIan hospitality for two weeks, then turned around and massacred
forty of their hosts. The Campbells were long-time enemies
of the MacDonalds, and there is no doubt that the abominable conspiracy was arranged in London by the two Campbell earls, Breadalbane and Argyll, along with Sir John
Dalrymple of Stair, King William's Scottish advisor. There
are still MacDonald homes in the Highlands today where
the name Campbell is a bad word.

The clan system had long been broken down and its
members dispersed by the time Sir Walter Scott wrote his
romantic books about them and Queen Victoria made the
Highlands a fashionable place to visit. The Jacobite rebellions of the eighteenth century with their terrible reprisals,
the Clearances, emigration, and the increase in sheep farming — all of these contributed to the end of the clan system.

Still the names remain and Clan Societies flourish, and
the children of Donald, Robert, Gregor, and others keep in
touch with each other from John o'Groats to Khatmandu.

Most visitors to Scotland, whether they can claim a clan
heritage or not, are familiar with tartans, the brightly
colored woolen fabrics that are the emblems of the various
clans. Sheep have been grazing on the green hillsides and
by the sparkling lochs for hundreds of years. The women
who long ago sat at spinning wheels wore animal skins
and homespun linens made from native flax, since the
lairds owned the sheep and undoubtedly got most of the
wool. For a long time only the wealthy wore woolen
garments.

It is safe to suppose that the first woolen materials were
rough in texture and drab in color, probably dirty white or

grey for the most part. But the Celts are a romantic race with imagination, and up in the Highlands and Islands they soon caught on to the use of vegetable dyes. They found they could get different colors from plants and came up with the following selection:

Blaeberries, currant bush tops, dulse, and lichens—*browns*
Alder bark and dock root—*black*
Cup moss—*purple*
Dandelion leaves—*magenta*
Blaeberries with club moss—*blue*
Wild cress—*violet*
Whin or gorse, broom, and knapweed—*greens*
Bracken and heather—*yellow*
White lichen—*red*

Indigo, another vegetable dye, was also imported from Holland from very early times. With the above materials the Highlanders got quite inventive and turned out brightly checkered material which we now know as tartan.

Tartan is what most Americans refer to as "plaid." A plaid as we know it in Scotland is actually a type of tartan shawl worn over one shoulder by someone in Highland dress. However, tartan material was called "plaiding," and long before it was made up into kilts, Highlanders wore an eighteen-foot-long plaid wrapped around the body and belted at the waist. Then someone came up with the clever idea of the kilt.

We do not know exactly when the first tartan material originated, although we do know that King James III's treasurer in his records of 1471 mentions "four elne and ane halve of tartane." We can be reasonably sure that some time before that tartan was used by a chieftain who wanted to be able to see who was on *his* side in a fight. All his boys wore it, and soon all of his enemies' boys were wearing other tartans of different color and design.

In tartans the color is always solid in the yarn, and the blending is achieved in the woven design. Dozens of traditional family tartans have evolved and have been passed on through generations in the form of "warping sticks," carefully marked with the number of threads of each color used across the warp and similarly in the weft.

Tartan is not, of course, the only woolen cloth woven in Scotland. Scotland is famous for other woolens and tweeds, and Harris tweed in particular is a name that spans the world.

The origin of the word *tweed* itself is interesting. It comes from "tweel" or "twill" (tweel being the vernacular) and denotes a heavy cloth formed in a twill pattern—two threads together crossing over and under two other threads. One day a couple of hundred years ago a London merchant wrote the word "tweel" in such a hurry that it came out looking like "tweed," and his cohorts read it that way. Since one of the centers of Scotland's woolen industry was then and is now in the Border country around a river called the Tweed, the spelling seemed very logical. So tweed it became and has remained.

Harris Tweed is defined by the National Association of Scottish Woollen Manufacturers as "a tweed from pure virgin wool produced in Scotland, spun, dyed and finished in the Outer Hebrides and hand-woven by the islanders at their own homes in the Islands of Lewis, Harris, Uist, Barra and their several purtenances and all known as the Outer Hebrides."

Harris Tweed, which the islanders call *Cló Mòr,* the Big Cloth, is a rather hairy, warm, and incredibly hard-wearing woolen material that retains a faint scent of the mosses used in its dyeing process. Like all other tweeds, it is meant to withstand wear in all weathers and for years has been worn by people working outdoors, like farmers, gamekeepers, fishermen, and shepherds. Sportsmen and women have, of course, also been wearing tweeds for a long time, and the typical picture of a hunter setting out on a Scottish deer hunt shows him in a tweed suit and a Sherlock-Holmes-type hat.

In the old days the women of Harris and the other islands used to tramp the tweed in buckets of water in order to shrink it, and there are still songs sung in Gaelic in the Hebrides today which are the old "waulking songs" of the early tweed industry. Now machines are used for shrinking ("fulling"), and the singing has been replaced with mechanical clatter.

The basics of the woolen industry, however, are still the same, and the old craft traditions of excellence remain. Today wool being manufactured is still treated with "considerable but respectful violence," as E. S. Harrison says in *Scottish Woollens*. Before we see a bolt of material in a shop it has already been through a multitude of processes. The fibers have been subjected to washing in hot alkaline solutions, dyeing, cropping, oiling, passing through teasing machines, carding, and spinning. Then the spun yarn has been woven and the cloth subjected to felting, finishing, final drying, steaming, and pressing. Phew!

In Scotland, as you might guess, little is wasted in the manufacture of woolens. All the wool can be used—even the coarsest, from the black-faced sheep, makes sturdy carpets. Scottish people make woolens; English people tend to make worsteds. The difference reflects again the thrift of the Scots. In the manufacture of worsteds, the wool is combed and all short hairs are removed, to leave fibers of the same length. In the manufacture of woolens, the wool is carded (processed between two flat boards covered with wire teeth), and *nothing* is removed. The yarns which result are quite different; the worsted is smooth like a miniature cable, while the woolen, after carding, is flat and tangled. A worsted suit is therefore likely to be fine and smooth and to have an attractive luster. But the wool suit is heavier and warmer and will not glaze as fast.

Since the nineteenth century many woolens have come in what is known as a "mixture,"—a subtle blending of colors like green and purple which makes "heather" tones. Other woolens fall into the category known to the industry as district checks. These checks are not complicated like tartans but are usually small checks of two or three different colors. Most of the district checks are based on the small quarter-inch black and white check of the Borders known as Shepherd Tartan—which was somebody's inconspicuous answer to the rowdier Highland tartans. This check was often woven into a plaid for local shepherds and served as overcoat, lunch bag, lamb carrier—whatever. The shepherd's plaid is traditionally four yards long and one and one half yards wide and is worn over one shoulder or wrapped around the body.

From the Shepherd Tartan evolved dozens of other small checks, many with delightful names like Glenurquhart, the Ballindalloch, the Wyvis ("ground is a deep fawn of the tint of withered bracken or dead beech leaves"), the Ardtornish, the Erchless, the Buccleuch, and many more.

A good weaver can turn out one hundred twenty-five yards of woolen material in a week. It is on record that one small Border village during World War I clothed four Scottish battalions every week—that is, they turned out fifteen thousand yards of tartan cloth a week for many weeks. A lot of that good tartan ended up on the bloody fields of Belgium and France, and the boys who wore it never came home. About one hundred fifty thousand Scots were killed in World War I.

What of the wool itself, the yarn spun in the cottage

industries of Scotland and in the great mills of the Lowlands and the Borders? Much of that wool is from Cheviot sheep, a breed originating in the hills between Scotland and England. Some wool comes from the small, active sheep of the Shetland Isles off Scotland's north coast. These islands used to belong to Norway but were pledged to King James III of Scotland as a dowry for his wife, Margaret of Norway, back in 1468. The sheep were presumably brought from Norway originally. Although the latitude of the Shetlands is the same as the southern tip of Greenland, their climate is very damp and mild, and frost and snow are rare. The coats of the sheep produce gossamer fine wool, which can be knitted into soft white shawls almost as fine as spider webs. The wool is so fine that a pound of it would stretch for ninety-five miles! Shetland woolens are certainly fine, both in texture and quality.

Between the Orkneys and the Shetlands lies a tiny island called Fair Isle, known for the exquisite patterns of its hand-knitted garments. Legend says that survivors of a Spanish galleon wrecked there after the Armada of 1588 taught the islanders how to form these patterns. They use bright colors intricately knitted into a fawn background, and for years it was fashionable for Lowland children to own Fair Isle sweaters, tams, and mittens.

In the Hillfoots area at the edge of Stirlingshire and Clackmannanshire, a large group of small manufacturers started knitwear businesses in the nineteenth century. This was the nucleus of the women's knitted garments industry in Scotland. Starting with woven tartan shawls in 1800, the businesses went on to socks, stockings, sweaters, gloves, mittens, and so forth. Towns like Alloa, Alva, Menstrie, Tillicoultry, and Tullibody were busy places through the first half of the twentieth century, their needles and knitting machines clacking furiously.

Down in the Borders they've been turning out Gala Tweels, Greys, and Blues for years—in fact, Galashiels established a Weavers Corporation back in 1666. Now towns all over what we call the Scott Country are turning out beautiful knitted garments as well. Scottish cashmeres are famous throughout the world.

Cashmere itself is not Scottish. Cashmere is the finest goat, sheep, and yak hair available in Asia, the very finest coming from China. Only the name comes from India and that has undergone a typical misspelling (Kashmir is the true name). Back in the nineteenth century cashmere brought fame to the town of Paisley outside Glasgow, which for seventy years produced thousands of Paisley shawls, woven from a mixture of cashmere, cotton, and silk, without one of which no Victorian lady's trousseau was complete. Now the cashmere is knitted into sweaters for ladies who still like to feel its incomparable softness and warmth. Companies like Ballantyne of Peebles, Pringle, Peter Scott, and others have been turning out sweaters to please customers all over the world for many years now. Ballantynes have also been mass-producing the diamond-patterned socks known as Argylls for more than fifty years. Many knitwear manufacturers, like McDougalls of Lanark, produce mainly for the export market and work closely with Continental designers to maintain high style standards.

Yet among all the knitwear, tweeds, and woolens manufactured in Scotland, tartan holds the honored place. There's a charisma about the kilt that makes visitors to Scotland thrill at the sight of a kilted Scot striding down the street. And a kilted Scotsman visiting the United States on business is likely to do better than ever on account of his kilt.

The kilt is specifically a Highland dress, and only about one-third of Scotland's inhabitants are technically entitled to wear it. But it was taken over by the Lowlanders probably as late as the seventeenth century and popularized by that great Lowlander, Sir Walter Scott. The kilt is still popular with many today, and it is recognized all over the world as the national dress of Scotland. Those who laugh at men in skirts should remember that Highland regiment referred to by its enemies as "the ladies from hell."

A poem by Neil Munro, called "The Kilt's My Delight," expresses some of the mystery and magic of the kilt:

> Wool from the mountain, dyes from the vale
> Loom in the clachan, peat fires bright;
> To every strand of it some old tale—
> Oh the tartan kilt is my delight!
> Went into its spinning brave songs of Lorn;
> Its hues from the herb and the berry were spilt;
> Lilts of the forest and glee of morn
> Are in his walking who wears the kilt!

A kilt is a grand garment—especially if you have the legs for it. It is warm and practical and great for walking. Bear in mind that the Scottish soldiers are basically infantry, not cavalry. To make a kilt, you need seven yards of tartan twenty-seven inches wide, and most of that material goes into the pleating; the pleats are stitched down over the hips to provide extra warmth for the kidneys. The kilt is a wrap-around garment with a plain front, belted at the side of the waist. The lower flap is fastened with a large silver pin. One thing the kilt *never* has is a hem. The lower edge is always formed from the selvage of the cloth, and the proper length is gauged as follows: if the kilt just barely touches the floor when the wearer is kneeling, then the length is exactly right. Long kilts look dreadful, and the worst thing that can happen is to have one which droops behind the back of the knees.

The kilt is (sorry, ladies) a *male* garment. Women properly wear a version of it called a kilted skirt which does not require as much material and is kinder to most feminine hips.

When fully dressed in daytime Highland dress, a man wears with the kilt a plain shirt and tartan tie, a rough tweed jacket, a sporran, woolen hose (knee-sock type), and brogues. The sporran is a purse suspended from chains, and it hangs at the lap. Sporrans come in different styles and are usually made of leather or fur—an Edinburgh firm turns out twenty thousand of them every year to suit all tastes. A man may also carry a dirk, or dagger, in his sock to ward off enemies or to open a can of sardines. On his head he can wear either a Balmoral bonnet (a type of tam) or a Glengarry (a hat shaped like an upturned rowboat with two ribbons hanging down behind). He may also wear a tartan plaid over one shoulder, fastened with a silver brooch.

For evening wear, Highland dress is one of the world's most splendid. Then the jacket may be of black, blue, or green velvet or velour cloth, with silver buttons, and the shirt has ruffles at the neck and cuffs. The kilt itself may be of finer material than the type of wool known as rank and file, or "R. & F. thin" used for regular wear. Shoes are shiny black with large silver buckles, and the sporran is made of a fine fur such as otter with silver trim. A gentleman wearing this fine apparel deserves an elegant partner in a long white dress with a silken tartan sash on her shoulder.

Now we come to the big question. When a man wears the kilt, what does he wear *under* it? Scotsmen all over the world may never forgive this disclosure. The truth is that most of them do wear something under the kilt—a small pair of matching tartan shorts, called trews.

But if you're in the army, that's a different story. You don't wear a thing under the kilt except yourself. And just in case you put on a pair of underpants by mistake, an officer with a cane flips up the kilt to check at inspection time. Or so the old story goes . . . .

The ancient cathedral of Glasgow, which shelters the crypt of Saint Mungo, patron saint of the city.

CHAPTER 4

DISTINCTLY SCOTTISH: RELIGION AND POLITICS

COMPARED WITH CHURCHES in the United States, churches in Scotland today are sadly empty. Still, statistics say that more Scots than English attend church, so perhaps Presbyterianism is more enduring than King Charles II had expected. Charles, who was pushing for Episcopalianism, declared back in the seventeenth century that Presbyterianism was "no fit religion for a Gentleman."

A century before Charles's outburst, the Protestant Reformation had come to both England and Scotland, bringing Episcopalianism to one and Presbyterianism to the other. John Knox, a leader of the new Presbyterian movement in Scotland, loudly and forcefully denounced the church in Rome. Since then, the Scots have been wary of things "Papist." Only about 15 percent of the Scots population today belongs to the Roman Catholic Church. The majority are Presbyterians, others Methodists (not as many as John Wesley would have wished after his twenty-two visits to Scotland), Episcopalians (an independent Scottish type, of course—what else?), a few Baptists, Mormons, and Jehovah's Witnesses. The large cities also have small Jewish communities.

Having weathered the storm of Covenanting in the seventeenth century, when three hundred Scots ministers took their congregations out on to the moors to worship in defiance of the Episcopalian English kings, the Kirk in Scotland continued to show itself ever ready to disagree when it saw fit. It was quite popular to secede on this issue, and by the early nineteenth century some interesting-sounding splits had been made. How about the Auld Lights, the New Lights, followed by the Auld Light Anti-Burghers and the New Light Anti-Burghers? History books tell us they were all split on "matters of conscience." The main issue of the day was supposedly that of patronage whereby many of the landed gentry had the authority to choose their local pastors. This went against the grain of the Presbyterians, who believed the pastors should be chosen by representatives of the congregation. But the real issue was moderation sneaking into a church that had never shown much desire to be moderate.

In 1843 the extent of secession within the Kirk was clearly displayed at the General Assembly, when one-third of the ministers present walked out. This move was called the Disruption. The new group formed the Free Kirk of Scotland, as opposed to the Old Kirk, and was disparagingly referred to in some circles as the "Wee Frees."

Today services in both the Free and Old churches are very similar. There is not much levity in either service, and the music is usually the grand and majestic type. Communion is celebrated only four times a year. Psalms and Paraphrases are regularly sung as well as hymns, and the minister rarely encourages the congregation to participate actively in the service. One enthusiastic English visitor of fundamental leanings, on visiting a Scottish church, called out "Hallelujah!" and "Praise the Lord!" He was hushed by a local elder and told firmly, "We dinna praise the Lord here, sir."

Church services are usually held at 11 A.M. and 6 P.M., although many churches have canceled their evening services in recent years. Church bells sound loudly every Sunday in towns and villages; some are still pulled by hand.

Throughout Scotland there are some interesting old churches and cathedrals built of grey stone, set squarely in green countryside. Edinburgh has several beautiful churches, as most tourists are aware, and every May the General Assembly of the Church of Scotland meets in Edinburgh's majestic Assembly Hall. Not many tourists are aware, however, of the old cathedrals of Dunkeld and Dunblane, or the graceful Church of the Holy Rude (Cross) in Stirling, where Mary, Queen of Scots, held up her infant son, James, for baptism in 1566. In the border country stand the ruins of the ancient abbeys of Melrose, Jedburgh, Dryburgh, and Kelso. Sweetheart Abbey was built by Devorgilla of Galloway back in the fourteenth century for her vacillating husband, John Balliol, who sat on the throne of Scotland for two years. The abbeys were despoiled during sixteenth-century raids by bandits living in the Border country and remain today as beautiful shells, memories of the past when the great Catholic orders from the Continent flourished in Scotland. Today, one of these old orders, the Benedictine, is represented still in the Highlands by a monastery at Fort Augustus at the head of Loch Ness. The monastery building is part modern, part early eighteenth-century fort.

The island of Iona, where Columba founded his Celtic Church more than fourteen hundred years ago, has been the home of the Iona Community since 1928. The church there was restored and presided over by the Reverend George MacLeod (now Lord MacLeod), and today it occupies a central part of Scotland's religious heritage, fulfilling Columba's own prophecy, made the day before he died:

> Small and mean though this place is, yet it shall be held in great and unusual honor, not only by Scotic kings and people, but also by rulers of foreign and barbarous nations, and by their subjects; the saints also, even of

other churches, shall regard it with no common reverence.

Iona is also the burial place of forty-eight Scottish kings, some of whom were not at all religious.

The keeping of the Sabbath, once a countrywide institution, has faded away in many communities with the popularity of driving, sports, and other recreations. (Although an Englishman once said that Scots kept the Sabbath—and anything else they could lay their hands on.) It is still fairly quiet in many Scottish towns on a Sunday, and old habits die hard. Not so long ago absolutely everything from shops to tennis courts was closed, and the only recreation possible was a decorous Sunday afternoon walk—very popular, for Scots are great walkers. Sunday drinking is now allowed, but drinking hours are rather limited. Another English wit has said that you can drink in Scotland before twelve noon but never after 11:00 P.M., times which are all right if you are an afternoon drinker.

Some Scots still maintain a schedule on Sundays very similar to that of their grandparents. They rise a little later than usual, eat a good sturdy breakfast, and go to church. (Or stay at home and read the Sunday papers.) In the afternoon, after another big meal, they take a walk or a drive and then spend a quiet evening at home in front of the television. They may even on rare occasions attend that rapidly diminishing institution, the evening worship service. Statistics show more and more clearly, however, that the average Scot is not a regular church-goer. If rebuked for this, he or she would be quite likely to repeat old Jock's words when his pastor remarked that he had not seen Jock in church lately: "Dinna worry, meenister—I'm tinkerin' awa' wi' my soul mysel'."

As for tartan politics, some of the same independent nature survives here too, in the form of the Scottish National

Party. Actually, if you live in Scotland, you have a choice of four different political parties. As in England, there are the Conservatives, who are still often called Unionists because their party supported the 1707 Union with England, the Labour Party, and the Liberals. But in Scotland there is also the Scottish National Party, which, in an era when many countries have forgotten their national identity, is not only surviving but positively thriving.

In the general election of 1974, the S.N.P. (Scottish National Party) gained a total of eleven seats, with 30.44 percent of the national vote. Only ten years before, the S.N.P. had no members in parliament and was polling a slender 2.4 percent of the vote.

What has caused this remarkable rise in Scottish National Party influence? Undoubtedly a growing disenchantment among Scots with the other political parties that have run the government for so long. The fact that in 1964 there were only fifteen Scottish National candidates opposing Labour and Conservative seats while in 1974 there were seventy-one S.N.P. candidates—one opposing every Labour and Conservative in the race—indicates a tremendous surge of interest in a national party.

Since the union of the Scottish and English parliaments in 1707, the government of Scotland has been managed from Westminster, London. There are, of course, separate Scottish departments for different aspects of its economic life (health, education, forestry, fisheries, and so forth), and since 1939 Saint Andrew's House in Edinburgh has housed them. There is also an appointed Scottish Secretary of State who is a member of the national cabinet. Scotland sends forty-five representatives to Westminster—there are five hundred English M.P.'s—and until 1974 these representatives were almost always Tories, Liberals, or Socialists. It is interesting to note, however, that of the two Communists ever elected to Parliament by popular vote, one of them, Willie Gallagher, came from East Fife, Scotland. Until recently, therefore, the system tended to maintain what amounted to an extension of English politics north of the border. And, in many cases, Scottish interests were subordinated to "national welfare."

With the increase in revenue from things Scottish, many Scots feel that they should receive a substantial increase in national benefits. For example, whisky provides one of the largest dollar amounts of revenue in the United Kingdom, but the S.N.P. feels that the amount of monetary return to Scotland is disproportionately low.

The fast-flowing rivers of northern Scotland have provided hydroelectric power to light up English towns for many years now, and Scots are complaining of rising electricity prices at home.

Now that supplies of underwater oil have been found in the North Sea off the east coast of Scotland, a new question arises: who is to benefit from the revenue from the oil—the national government in Westminster, or the Scots in Scotland? By 1980 the enormous prosperity flowing into the Aberdeen area could spread throughout the country, bringing oil self-sufficiency not only to Scotland, but also to the whole of Britain. Scottish Nationalists say, "Stop it at the border," but it is not so easy, as politicians from all parties will explain. Millions of dollars have been poured into the oil production in the North Sea by many different countries, and when Scotland participated in the 1964 Oil Treaty, it was participating alongside England as part of the unit of Great Britain. A whole new treaty would have to be set up and ratified in order to change the way things are going— or change the way the oil is flowing.

But the Scottish National Party sees this as a good opportunity to break away from England, form its own government in Edinburgh, and administer Scotland from there. The S.N.P. members are convinced they can do a better job for the Scots without further close involvement with Westminster. Although they plan to maintain good relations with their neighbor, they also wish to establish an independent place for themselves in the United Nations, the British Commonwealth, and the Common Market of Europe.

The S.N.P. believes basically in the open plebiscite, and on the Common Market question, for example, the party would have put the matter to general vote before making such an enormous commitment on behalf of the country.

Scottish nationalism had its beginnings as a political party in 1853, in the foundation of a venerable-sounding institution, the National Association for the Vindication of Scottish Rights. From 1886 to 1928 there was an active Scottish Home Rule Association, formed by those of all parties, but mostly supported by Liberals and later on by Labour members. Early Labour Party leaders, Keir Hardie and Ramsay Macdonald in particular (both Scots), were keen supporters of Home Rule for Scotland. In 1928 Cunningham Graham became the first leader of the Scottish Party, and soon the party could boast of famous writers like Compton Mackenzie and Hugh McDiarmid in its ranks.

In 1934 the title Scottish National Party was adopted, and there was great hope that Home Rule for Scotland would eventually be realized—especially since that concept was actually written into the Labour Party Manifesto and remained there until 1945. Now the S.N.P. has hopes that one day again that policy will be rewritten into the Labour Party policy.

Not much was heard from the Nationalists in the fifties and sixties. But in 1950 a small but enthusiastic group of student S.N.P. members very cleverly removed the Stone of Scone (pronounced "Scoon") from the position it enjoyed under the Coronation Throne in Westminster Abbey. The Stone of Scone was the traditional stone on which Scottish kings had been crowned from time immemorial. Somehow the students whisked the stone out of the Abbey, loaded it into a car, and were up and over the border before they were caught. They made an historically accurate claim, by the way, that the stone belonged to Scotland and that Edward I had no right to it when he removed it some eight hundred years before. Their objections were overruled, and the Stone was returned to Westminster.

Three years later, when Queen Elizabeth was crowned, there was some heated discussion in Scotland with regard to her title, Queen Elizabeth II. Since the union of the crowns of Scotland and England did not take place until after the death of Good Queen Bess, Scotland never had a Queen Elizabeth I, and therefore the present Queen is, strictly speaking, Queen Elizabeth I of Scotland.

Gallup-type polls show that today only a minority of Scots favor total independence with a clear break from England. The polls do show, however, that a majority of Scots favor limited self-government with a Scots Parliament seated at Edinburgh. Now that oil has been found off Scottish shores, the feeling that Scotland "can afford" self-government is running high.

The University of Edinburgh, one of Scotland's oldest, was founded in 1583.

CHAPTER 5

MATTERS OF PRIDE: EDUCATION AND LAW

IF YOU WERE TO ASK a Scot to name the greatest thing about his or her country, the answer would probably be: "Its beauty." And after that you might hear, "Its education." Education has been important to the Scots from very early times, even when schools were a rare commodity all over Europe.

The town of Stirling is a good example. Stirling today is a busy market town of some thirty thousand people, set in lovely fertile farmland watered by the River Forth. Its castle sits high on a volcanic cone that thrusts upward above the plain, and historians say that there has been a town there possibly since Roman times. Today Stirling has several excellent schools and a high school with a proud record of former students. But back in the twelfth century Stirling had a school too. An ancient parchment tells us that a certain Bishop of Saint Andrews gave to Queen Margaret's Church of the Holy Trinity of Dunfermline, the churches of Perth and Stirling "and their schools."

Little else is known about Stirling's twelfth-century school, save that it was administered by the Church and that its teachers were monks. But by the fifteenth century Scotland had established three universities (Saint Andrews in 1411, Glasgow in 1451, and Aberdeen in 1494) and was sending young men to college at home and overseas. Undoubtedly some of these students came from Stirling's "grammar school," which was by that time a thatched, one-story house.

Imagine Jimmy Johnstone as he might have been as a student at that grammar school. Jimmy lived in Stirling and his father was on the "Toon Cooncil" (Town Council), so Jimmy went to the grammar school which the Council helped the Church administer. Since Jimmy was one of the "tounis bairnes" (town children), the fee his father paid for his schooling was modest, although Jimmy might have doubted the worth of it some cold mornings as he climbed the cobblestones of the Castle Hill at 6 A.M. School was held every day except Sunday from six until six, and Jimmy went home for breakfast and dinner in the middle of the day. Sunday was not much of a holiday either, for he had to sit through two long sermons in Church and repeat his Catechism in good order.

The one thing Jimmy could look forward to was a holy day or saint's day, which all Scottish students enjoyed until after the Reformation of the church, when those days were arbitrarily struck off the Protestant calendar.

Jimmy Johnstone was enrolled in the grammar school at the age of eight and began learning Latin immediately. The headmaster of the school, known as the Master or the Dominie (from Latin "magister Artium" and "dominus") taught him Latin grammar for three years. The Doctor, the Master's assistant, also taught Latin, as well as arithmetic and writing. Jimmy's fourth year in school was spent learning Latin verse, including the Psalms, and by his fifth year his horizons had widened to include writers like Erasmus, Virgil, Terence, Horace, and others. Most fun of all, he began to *debate* in Latin!

When the first Education Act was passed by the Scottish Parliament in 1496, Jimmy was not affected by it, because he was already in school. The Act compelled "country gentlemen" to send their sons first to grammar school "till they have perfyte Latin" and then to university for "instruction in the law." Jimmy's father, who was a wealthy merchant, wanted his son to be a lawyer and considered sending him to either Utrecht or Leyden to study. But Jimmy eventually went up to the university at Glasgow, became a Magister Artium, and went on to teach Latin to more small boys.

By the end of the sixteenth century Scotland had added Edinburgh to its list of universities and now boasted four to England's two. This was really a fantastic achievement for a country the size of Scotland whose population at that time was well under a million people.

And the Scots owe a lot of their emphasis on education to that doughty old gentleman, John Knox, who was one of the leaders of the Scottish Reformation. Although Knox came out against that "monstrous regiment of women," he may be partially forgiven on the grounds that he also wrote *The Buke of Discipline* in 1560, a book which provided a sturdy foundation for the Scottish educational system.

Knox stated that, "Seeing that God hath determined that his Church here on earth shall be taught not by angels but by men" (another dig at the Catholic Church), there should be:

(1) a school at every church
(2) a schoolmaster to teach grammar and Latin in every village
(3) a college teaching Greek, Latin, logic, and rhetoric in every "notable town"
(4) help for poor boys and girls (yes, he said girls!) to attend the above schools
(5) encouragement for all "fit to study" to attend the university
(6) education of "rich and potent" children to be at parents' expense.

Not content with this, Knox went on to say that "children of the poor must be supported and sustained on the charge of the Church till trial be taken whether the spirit of docility be found in them or not"!

Using this as a general guide, therefore, the Scots made education more available to children of the poor and lower middle classes in their country than anywhere else in Europe. It was a Scots family's pride that their children could read and write, and a poor university student might go off to his studies with his bag of oatmeal to sustain him for the term, convinced that whatever sacrifice he or his family was making would be more than worthwhile in the end.

In 1696 the Act for the Settling of Schools informed all Scottish landowners that if there was no school in their parish, they had better look to their bank accounts and build one. Moreover, it was up to them to pay their dominie not less than thirteen dollars a year, or more than twenty-seven, lest he grow spoiled. Over and above this money, the dominie received about a dollar a year for each pupil, and some of his pupils might pay him with peats for the schoolroom fire.

By the eighteenth century, Scottish universities had won international acclaim. Teaching in Latin had been replaced by teaching in English, and the regent system had been abolished. For the first time, professors were established for separate subjects, and students studied under different men throughout their university careers, instead of remaining with one regent constantly for all subjects. Edinburgh became the medical center of Europe. The Royal College of Physicians, founded in 1681, had laid the foundations, and the College of Surgeons had received a charter from James IV some 170-odd years earlier. By the eighteenth century students were pouring into Scotland. They studied under such famous doctors as John Hunter, the founder of pathological anatomy, and his brother William, an obstetrician. At Glasgow Adam Smith, the product of a good grammar school, was sounding out his new doctrine of economics from his *Wealth of Nations,* namely that the state should not interfere in economic affairs.

In the nineteenth century Scotland sent twice as many students to universities as did England, its wealthier neighbor. By the time the Education Act of 1872 was passed, which made education compulsory for all children between the ages of five and thirteen in both countries, Scotland could sit back with a smug smile: 80 percent of Scottish children were already in school. While the fact that 1 child in 140 went on to secondary school may not seem impressive at first glance, compare it with Prussia's 1 in 249 and France's 1 in 570. In England, where the Industrial Revolution was cutting down drastically on the school population and filling the factories and mines with working children, only 1 child in 1,300 received more than an elementary education.

What was happening back in Stirling? The advance of the universities had encouraged the grammar schools to forge ahead and introduce new subjects. Jimmy Johnstone's great-great-great-(and several more greats) grandchildren were learning modern languages like French and German, although the classics were still popular at Stirling High School. Students also enjoyed new subjects like bookkeeping, drawing, and gymnastics; one enterprising master taught practical mathematics through land surveying.

In 1854 the foundation stone of a new high school building was laid on Academy Road, Stirling, and according to a local newspaper, "Not even when Royalty graced our ancient town was there ever witnessed a finer spectacle than that which was seen this third of August at the laying of the foundation stone of a school."

By 1863 there were 373 students at Stirling High, and 146 of them were girls. The fact that Scottish education was coeducational from an early date is one of its more remarkable aspects. As far back as 1694 a mistress was appointed by the Stirling Town Council to teach girls housewifery; among the tasks to be taught included making "seed and plumb cakes for funeralls and other occasions," "the suing of white and colloured seams," and "washing and dressing."

Coeducation did not, however, extend to the universities until the late nineteenth century, when the presence of women on the campus must surely have disturbed the equilibrium of several stately professors. Since then the percentage of women in the liberal arts field has risen well beyond that of men, and more are studying medicine and the sciences every year.

Elementary and high schools have become more "modern," and many now offer facilities that their students' grandparents would have thought impossible—and even unnecessary. Private, fee-paying schools continue to hold a small place in Scotland's educational system. The very small ones have largely been eliminated by the cost of living squeeze. Some of those remaining are the equivalent of the English "public schools"—boarding schools that offer moderately good education with high snob appeal. One of the most famous is probably Gordonstoun in the north, alma mater of Prince Philip and Prince Charles. Many of the larger towns saw new schools established during the eighteenth and nineteenth centuries. Wealthy merchants endowed several schools in Edinburgh, Glasgow, and other towns, and these schools have always enjoyed excellent educational ratings.

In 1967 Scotland added its first university in five hundred years. The University of Stirling is a modern campus in a beautifully wooded estate between Stirling and Bridge of Allan and houses about thirty-four hundred students. Already it has more students than the oldest university, Saint Andrews.

In Scotland, scholarships to university are known as "bursaries"—from the French *bourse,* meaning "purse." More and more students are now receiving bursaries, and there has been controversy recently as to the value of the present system. The rapid rise in the cost of living since World War II has taken away the independence of the universities and made them government supported. There is now a tendency towards uniformity of education at the university level throughout Britain, which is troubling many Scots. After all, they have always felt a cut above England in education—and they would like it to stay that way.

A Scottish farmer once asked a student if he was studying for the ministry. "Oh no, sir," replied the student. "I'm not going to be a minister—I'm going to be a lawyer." "Man, man," said the farmer, "jist the opposite."

For many years justice in Scotland, as in most other countries, was the justice of the sword, the mailed fist, and the strong right arm—and possession was certainly nine points of the law. This heritage persisted perhaps longer than in many other countries, however, because of the continuation of the feudal system as it was practiced in the Highlands. There the clans maintained a justice of their own, by which any member of a clan could be called to account for the crimes of a fellow member. This naturally tended to keep vendettas going from generation to generation, and these vendettas were many.

One bloody story concerns the Appin Stewarts and the MacLarens, who were ever battling with their enemies the MacDougalls and the MacFarlanes. It is retold here from the 1972 *Highland Diary and Yearbook:*

The green turf at the head of the Glen of Orchy lay piled with the bodies of fallen Stewarts and their MacLaren allies. Nor had their enemies, the combined forces of the MacDougalls and MacFarlanes, fared well. For although they had won the day, they had lost so many men to the Stewart and MacLaren broadswords that they were never again to be the powerful force in Argyll which they had been until this day.

The Chief of the MacFarlanes wandered among the fallen. A dying MacLaren called to him for a drink from a nearby well and as this charitable soul bent over the well to comply with his enemy's request, the MacLaren drew his bow taut and sent an arrow through his back. The MacFarlane groped behind him to feel for the arrow.

"Search in front of you," called the MacLaren, exulting in the penetration of his shaft, "Search in front of you and you will find it."

The cause of this bloody battle was the murder about ten days previously of Sir John Stewart, Lord of Lorn, by Alan MacDougall. Sir John, an aging widower without legitimate male issue, had sent for his natural son Dugald in order that he might marry his mother and legitimize Dugald's inheritance of the lordship. A bizarre situation, but one which was by no means unusual in those days.

As the wedding party approached, the MacDougalls, who had a vested interest in ensuring that Dugald did not inherit, fell upon Sir John and inflicted mortal wounds. The wedding was rushed through just before he died, leaving young Dugald an inheritance whose legality was, perhaps understandably, in question and with the murder of his father to avenge.

But the Highlands were not alone in their lawlessness.

Some of the bloodiest feuds of all time were perpetrated in the Borders, where a long history of sheep and cattle thieving and other crimes made the establishment of a formal judicial system very difficult. In the Borders the early "justiciaries" were the Wardens, put there by the Scottish and English governments to maintain at best a kind of truce—even when the two countries were not actively at war. The wardens' job was complicated by a great deal of inter-marrying among the families on both sides of the Border, thus developing dangerous alliances and promoting raids by large bands of men. These men were the infamous Border raiders, or reivers, the first gangsters and inventors of the word "blackmail." They exacted blackmail (*mail* meaning payment or rent) for protection from their pillage. When they weren't raiding for sheep, they were out looking for women, and many Elliots, Armstrongs, Grahams, and the like made interracial marriages—that is, with English girls from across the Marches.

So much for the Highlands and the Borders. What about the Lowlands? As late as the eighteenth century, when Dr. Samuel Johnson visited Scotland and asked a learned mini-ster which clans were the most savage, he was told, "Those that live next the Lowlands"—so the Lowlands must have had their moments too, in order to have caused a remark like that.

Justices of the peace were established in Scotland in the late sixteenth century, and by the time James Dalrymple, Viscount of Stair, came along in the seventeenth century, the Scottish legal system was at least definable. In 1681 Dalrymple wrote *The Institutions of the Law of Scotland,* a mighty tome still referred to today in Scottish law courts.

These courts are divided up as follows:

1) Magistrates Courts, presided over by baillies, who handle lesser cases like small claims and petty thefts.

2) Sheriff Courts, where the "sheriffs" (all professional
lawyers) handle all crimes except the highest like murder, treason, rape, and incest. There are twelve sheriff
courts, and the highest sentence a sheriff can hand out
is two years. The derivation of the word *sheriff* is *shire
reeve,* the "boss man" of the area.

3) High Court, which gives out more severe sentences. It
travels where needed.

4) Supreme Court, or Court of Session, presided over by
fifteen judges, who are senators from the College of
Justice.

Here's one story told about a case to be sent to magistrates court: Two farmers were fighting over the owner-
ship of some sheep, and they happened to consult two
lawyers who had offices next door to each other. After the
farmers had left the lawyers got together. "This business
about the sheep, Jamie," one of them said, "is surely something we can benefit from. I don't know about the animals,
but you can fleece one farmer, and I'll fleece the other!"

In Scotland the title "barrister" is not used. Scottish barris-
ters are "advocates." "Solicitors" are lawyers who work
mostly out of court, and some of them belong to an august
and ancient body, Writers to the Signet. You may still read
on a lawyer's door the title "Writer," which usually doesn't
mean he's an author.

An important man in Scots law is the procurator fiscal,
or crown counsel. He is the gentleman who receives all
reports of crimes from the police and who then decides
which court they should be tried in. The police themselves
do not prosecute. The procurator fiscal is appointed; he is
not elected, as many American police and court officials are.

Some Scottish lawyers will tell you today that Scots law
is an ideal combination of Anglo-American law (the pre-
cedent system and parliamentary acts) and ancient Roman

law (the principles that govern all lawmaking). Others will say that the present structure of society calls for reform of the civil laws in many cases and that the small exclusive body of lawyers at the top should be making some moves in that direction.

For a country that seems very uptight about many things, Scotland has held a remarkably "modern" view of divorce for a long time. Since the sixteenth century Scots have allowed divorce on the grounds of adultery or desertion. Lately the desertion period has been shortened to three years. Divorce today is also allowed on grounds of "cruelty, unnatural vice, and incurable insanity."

Scots law differs in several ways from English, the most outstanding difference perhaps being the third verdict. English courts, like American ones, have "Guilty" and "Not Guilty." Scottish courts have also "Not Proven," which means that there was insufficient evidence. A flippant explanation of this verdict might be "Not Guilty—but don't do it again."

One of the most famous trials in Scotland's history ended with a verdict of "Not Proven." One Madeleine Smith was accused in 1857 of the poisoning of her lover. Madeleine, a young woman from a respectable Glasgow family, was accused of administering poison to her French lover, L'Angelier, in order to regain possession of certain passionate letters which could have ruined her coming marriage to an older man of high social standing. That coming marriage, of course, never happened—after a trial of nine days' wonder that shook the Victorian establishment. But Madeleine survived to marry another and lived to a prosperous old age.

Thirty years before the trial of Madeleine Smith, something ghastly had happened in Edinburgh—something so ghastly that people walking down the West Port of Edinburgh on a dark night can still feel the evil of it. Two men called Burke and Hare murdered, over a period of nine months, sixteen people. The men then sold the bodies to a university surgeon for anatomical research. Burke and Hare were the body-snatchers of Robert Louis Stevenson's famous story, the so-called Resurrectionists, who in order to fill the needs of science were quite prepared to do murder for ten pounds per corpse. The receiver of their wares was a Dr. Robert Knox, a famous and popular anatomy professor who in his desire to have specimens for autopsy, closed his one good eye to what he must certainly have known.

The trial of Burke and Hare began on Christmas Eve 1828 and went on for twenty-four hours, the accused being defended at no cost to themselves by capable members of the Scots Bar. Burke was hanged, his carcass publicly anatomized (tickets being required for the event), his hide tanned, and his skeleton preserved in Edinburgh University's Anatomical Museum. Hare got off by a technicality, escaped the angry mob, and fled to London. There, rumor says, he fell into a limestone trench and was blinded. Dr. Knox was eventually digraced, lost his following, and his position, and died in poverty in London. The Edinburgh public reduced the ghastly incident to rhyme:

> Up the close and doun the stair
> But and ben wi' Burke and Hare.
> Burke's the butcher, Hare's the thief,
> Knox the boy that buys the beef.

Scots law tends to put the rights of the individual before the rights of the state, and in capital offenses tends to favor mercy. There were, for example, no executions in Scotland between the years 1929 and 1945, although there must have been capital crimes. Today the death penalty is pronounced for second murders, or killing of prison guards or police officers.

Some land laws in Scotland still have a feudal ring. For example, the very expression "feu duty"— the right of the laird to levy a small tax on property. This feu duty is today slowly being abolished, but the lairds still maintain certain local rights. For instance, a few years ago a Scot returning from Canada made arrangements to build a large house for his family on an estate overlooking the Firth of Forth. He was informed that he would have to consult the local laird as to the type of roof he could put on his house, and that the last word would certainly have to be the laird's. So he built his house, and the laird picked out the roof.

The police force in Scotland has a good reputation for politeness and efficiency. Each county has its own police department, and cooperation among departments is fluid. Rumor has it that, like the Irish cops in New York, many of the best London policemen are Scotsmen. And a certain large Canadian city several years ago fired the bulk of its police force because they were "on the take" and then recruited replacements in Scotland.

Not only fiction but fact has it that many leading lights in Scotland Yard are Scottish inspectors. Talking about Scotland Yard—why *Scotland* Yard? That famous institution known around the globe has its origins in a piece of land given to a tenth-century King of Scots as a place for him to stay when he came down to pay homage to the English king. The land, however, proved rather far from home to hold any lasting attraction for the Scottish kings, and homage was never anything they cared to keep up for very long anyway. But the site retained the name Scotland Yard and was first used for government buildings in the seventeenth century. The police moved in later, and the metropolitan police force of London (formed in 1829 from "the peelers" of Sir Robert Peel) made it their headquarters. Since then it has expanded in form and fame until the name Scotland Yard has become synonymous with crime-fighting.

The Scots on the whole are a law-abiding people. Surely part of this derives from their Calvinistic background, which has an ingrown respect for other people's property—unless, perhaps, that property happens to be game. There's an old proverb that says, "Taking a salmon from the river, a tree from the forest, and a deer from the mountain are three actions no Gael was ever ashamed of." Guns have not been a problem. Every gun owner is required to have a license, and most guns used are the hunting variety. All British police, which includes Scots, are reluctant to use guns and do not as a rule carry them.

Glasgow, Scotland's largest metropolitan area, has always had its fair share of crime. For years Argyll Street was famous for its bottle fights on Saturday nights, especially if there had been a big "fitba' match" (soccer game) earlier in the day. Perhaps Glasgow's crime rate can be at least partially accounted for by the city's mixed population. Among others, thousands of Irish moved into Glasgow in the nineteenth and twentieth centuries, and if there's one thing an Irishman and a Scotsman have in common, it's the fact they both dearly love a fight.

The crime rate in Scotland has risen during recent years, in accordance with crime rates in other countries. And percentage-wise, the capital crimes in Scotland are more frequent than most Scots would like to admit when they look at the overall picture for the whole island. Yet, in Britain as a whole in 1975 there were only thirty-seven murders. In California there were fifteen hundred. In Scotland a person has to use something other than a gun to dispose of an enemy. Let us hope things will continue like this. An angry Scot without a gun is dangerous enough!

The royal palace of Falkland is one of many castles that trace Scotland's notable history of architecture.

CHAPTER 6

A VISIBLE HERITAGE: ART AND ARCHITECTURE

SCOTLAND HAS ITS SHARE OF ancient dwellings, and there are several different types which tourists and students may visit.

The earliest inhabitants left nothing except graves and middens (garbage heaps) for later people to explore, and from these archeologists can tell a little about early times. For example, the first settlers camped around the coasts, and we know that their diet was shellfish and deer with some wolf and bear thrown in. These early people probably came from Ireland in the Stone Age. At first they lived like nomads along the west and northwest coasts of Scotland and then settled down to farm by the time the late Stone Age came along. The guess is that they spoke a language called Q-Celtic, so named because of the frequent use of the q sound, much later changed to c and k.

Then at least two separate groups came to Scotland. One group were long-headed people who were originally from the Mediterranean area. They settled in Brittany, Cornwall, Wales, and western and northwestern Scotland. We know that they buried their dead collectively in long graves, placing stone cairns over them. We know also that they were farmers who burned their land between crops, because we have found layers of ash in their farmlands, and that they raised sheep and cattle.

About 1600 B.C. another group began filtering into the

country from Holland and the Rhineland and settled at the head of the Forth and Tay firths. They were a round-headed people who buried their dead individually in stone-lined tombs over which they placed small cairns called "barrows." Because they put a drinking vessel inside the tomb, they have come to be called the Beaker Folk.

Smaller groups, who may have been offshoots of the Beaker people, but who burned their dead, moved into the Lothians later. Then, by 300 B.C., iron-using people moved up from England and France, who left us not only their tombs, but also actual dwellings that are still in existence today.

Perhaps the most famous remnant of Iron Age culture in Scotland is the village of Skara Brae in the Orkneys. This village is composed of stone houses and actual furnishings like built-in stone beds, hearths, and storage areas—all retrieved from sands which had covered and preserved them for hundreds of years.

It is believed that most early dwellings were made of perishable materials like wood and turf, but at Skara Brae the stone has given them permanence. Since there are no trees in Orkney, perhaps Skara Brae is merely a stone replica of what elsewhere would have been built with perishable materials.

The Iron Age produced other types of dwellings, such as forts or duns, which are fairly common; there are remains in various Scottish districts. The most striking type of building of the time was a tall, round stone tower dating from about 100 B.C. These towers are known as *brochs,* a Gaelic word which means "fortified dwelling." The best preserved broch is at Mousa in the Shetland Islands.

It is hard to imagine living in the broch of Mousa or spending much time in it, because it has no windows and must have been lit via an opening at the top. The tapering walls are double-thick, two-layered stone, standing about sixty feet high with a diameter of approximately sixty feet at the base. The rooms of the broch are at ground level only, and the one small doorway leads into a narrow passage defended by small cells on either side.

Remains of about four hundred and fifty brochs have been found on fertile land in Caithness, Orkney, Shetland, and the Hebrides, and it is safe to assume that they were used for strongholds and lookouts. Other scraps of civilization like stone querns, which were used for grinding grain, and shards of pottery have been found near the brochs, and the supposition is that there were groups of dwellings in the same area at one time.

There are two theories about the people who built the brochs. One is that the brochs were built by people who came and settled around 100 A.D. But the other theory is even more interesting. It puts forward the idea that the brochs were actually built by settlers *before* that time who were conquered by the later Picts (the Romans' painted men) and whose civilization was either demolished or assimilated into the newer one. This last certainly seems possible, since brochs are not found in the southern part of Scotland at all, whereas Pictish dwellings are found well into the south. Thus the Picts we talk about were probably a mixture of an even earlier ancient people. Contrary to the Gaels of the west who spoke Q-Celtic, they spoke P-Celtic (changed the q sound to p sound), and it is believed, although not positively known, that the two languages were distinct and different.

These Celts, or Picts, lived in earth-houses, or what have been called "souterrains," and there are several which can be visited in the counties of Fife, Angus, and Perth.

In 1949 a farmer found the most complete souterrain yet discovered in his field at Ardestie, between Dundee and

Arbroath, and another was found later that same year about
a mile from Ardestie. These earth-houses were originally
excavated so that they are partly below ground level. The
inhabitants lined the walls and floors with stones, and they
built doorways and drains. The souterrain near Ardestie,
christened Carlungie I, even has a shellfish tank, and there
are blackened hollows where ancient fires burned. Various
objects like stone molds and lamps were also found at
Carlungie I, and one of the most important was a Roman
amphora, a two-handled vase, which dates the souterrain
between A.D. 100 and 400.

Another ancient site visitors enjoy is the remains of the
Roman camp at Callander. Near the grounds of the charming Roman Camp Hotel are several circular mounds of
earth. One mound in particular was obviously artificially
constructed; it is called *Tom-ma-chessaig,* or the hill of
Saint Kessaig, after a Celtic saint. Two miles beyond Callander on the Kilmahog road lies the Dun of Bochastle,
which is the remains of an ancient fort.

In Dunipace, Stirlingshire, on the banks of the River
Carron, there are several large mounds which may have
been built when the Romans made a third-century peace
with the Picts. In which case, *Dunipace* means "the hill of
peace." On the other hand, many believe mounds like these
to be ancient Celtic burial grounds. In which case the Gaelic
name *Duinna-Bais* would apply, meaning "hills of death."
Mounds of this type are not uncommon in rural areas, and
visitors will be interested to find that although many centuries have passed, people have avoided building on or near
them whenever possible.

Another example of old dwellings in Scotland, not as
ancient, but interesting anyway, is the Farm Town of
Auchindrain in Argyllshire. In 1964 a trust was formed to
conserve the township of Auchindrain as a museum of

farming life, and today the village appears exactly as it did in the nineteenth century. The former tenants of Auchindrain paid rent to the Duke of Argyll and then drew lots to decide who would get which strips of land to cultivate. The land around Auchindrain has been under cultivation for hundreds of years. In fact it is probable that people have lived there for perhaps two thousand years, because there is a late Stone Age tomb close by as well as a large mound which could date from the Iron Age.

Today you can walk through the Weaver's Cottage, the School House, the Stoner's house, and other buildings, where old implements and furniture are on display—or you can walk along a rough track to the Wise Woman's house, whose garden is filled with herbs and medicinal plants.

The Scots are proud of their rural heritage and their beginnings, which were often scraped from an inhospitable soil, and they are making an effort to preserve that heritage.

Except for the ancient brochs and souterrains, other early buildings in Scotland with remains we can examine today are of later origin and primarily ecclesiastical in purpose. While monks formed the beautiful Book of Kells on the island of Iona, their stonemason brothers built a small, round church. On several islands off the west coast are remains of similar "beehive" churches, built by early settlers from Ireland. Because of the Irish settlers, early Scottish and Irish churches have a lot in common. The stone Celtic cross, so common in Ireland, is found in ancient Scottish graveyards yet. It is a unique design, a cross with a circle around the center. Look for examples in central Argyllshire and Kintyre.

Three of the best known of Scotland's ancient cathedrals —Saint Andrews, Elgin, and Glasgow—were all built prior to the Wars of Independence—that is, prior to the thirteenth and fourteenth centuries, and as such owe nothing in design to their English contemporaries. The design is simple and severe, but Glasgow has a very fine vaulted crypt which houses the shrine of Saint Mungo, the city's saint. Saint Andrews Cathedral, which took one hundred fifty years to build, was torn apart by a Reformation mob in three days as they vented their spite on the local churches. Now it remains a beautiful grey ruin with grass growing among its foundations.

After the Wars of Independence, architecture in Scotland was influenced more strongly by outside factors, and these factors were by and large English and French. The Normans, who, after their successful conquest in 1066, had built their own style of buildings all over England and made an institution out of the square Norman tower, were slower in impressing the Scots. At least fifty years elapsed before much Norman influence infiltrated Scots architecture, but eventually it came, and today we find examples like the tower of Dunblane Cathedral, which is alien to the remainder of the building and was probably built in the early 1100s.

Queen Margaret, wife of King Malcolm Canmore, was responsible for a great many changes in eleventh-century Scotland, including its architecture. Since she had grown up in a Norman court before marrying her wild Scotsman, she was accustomed to certain refinements which she introduced to her adopted country. She was undoubtedly responsible for certain modifications in housing; interior decorating, such as it was, became more lavish at her court, with the introduction of tapestries and silver tableware. The church Malcolm built for her at Dunfermline is not Celtic in design but noticeably French.

Other abbeys of Scotland also show a French influence, which is understandable, since many of the great monastic orders originated in France, and the monks moved to Scotland from the Continent. Melrose Abbey, built in the fifteenth century and ransacked by Border raiders in the sixteenth, is quite French in design. Other interesting monastic ruins are at Arbroath on the Fife coast and Cambuskenneth on the banks of the River Forth. Cambuskenneth has a tall tower standing today amid ruined foundations and houses the bones of King James III and his queen.

Since it is very hard to go far anywhere in Scotland without bumping into a castle or stately home—known to the locals as "the big house"—visitors are always interested in romantic tales of history. As in other countries, castles in Scotland were originally built purely for defense purposes, and at the beginning they were the simplest of dwellings. You needed a thick wall between yourself and your enemies, and you needed a lookout to keep track of what they were doing. Consequently you built a tall tower on a hill somewhere. Before stone was commonly used—and it was not in common use in Scotland until after 1300—people used timber to build their towers and fortified buildings. After Marco Polo brought gunpowder to Europe from China, it was gradually put to use in stone quarries, and stone became a convenient building material. Designs also became more complicated, and soon the simple tower was girdled with stone walls which encircled additional buildings like kitchens, stables, and armories. Dirleton Castle, built in 1225, looks almost like a castle on the French Loire, and it is one of the first stone castles in Scotland.

By the fifteenth century the French influence was responsible for the introduction of the long gallery, a fine example of which was built in 1461 at Falkland Palace. Also by the fifteenth century, the upper walls of many castles had piecrust-type frills known as crenellated parapets, with spaces in between where a handy cannon might be rested.

By the sixteenth and seventeenth centuries, Renaissance style courtyards with impressive gateways were appearing, and Sir William Bruce, an early Scottish architect, was redesigning buildings like Holyroodhouse and building new ones like Hopetoun House near Edinburgh. Hopetoun House has gardens like those of Versailles and was later rebuilt and expanded by the Adam family—William and his two sons, James and Robert.

The Adams, father and sons, but particularly sons, were world famous in the eighteenth century. They were part of a prosperous Edinburgh family, prosperous enough at least to send their sons on the "Grand Tour," which kept Robert two years on the Continent and sent him home with ideas he would never have picked up in his native Edinburgh. His designs resulted in beautiful homes with straight classical lines and interiors with exquisitely molded ceilings, fireplaces, and friezes. The Adam men did not confine their talents to Scotland but built stately homes south of the border also. They became the most popular architects of their day as well as the richest. Thanks to their genius we enjoy places like Mellerstain in Berwickshire, with its Italian gardens, and Culzean Castle in Ayrshire, with its beautiful plaster ceilings and grand staircase.

Looking at Charlotte Square in Edinburgh today, an observer may safely say, "It's Georgian," since the Adam elegant style has acquired that name over the years.

The Adams, father and sons, were part of the group of several great Scots who gave rise to the expression "Silver Renaissance," for in the eighteenth century Scotland was enjoying a period unprecedented in its history when it was leading Europe in the fields of medicine, architecture, economics, mathematics, and scientific inventions. Suddenly the upper classes in Scotland had a surfeit of capital to sponsor and endow, much of which went into building and research.

From Adam elegance, we come now to a term "Scots

Baronial," which, when pronounced, is often accompanied by a smirk. Balmoral Castle on Deeside, where the present Queen and her family spend several weeks each year, is a glorious example of this style. It is a co-mingling of towers, turrets, and tartan. The style originated from the early single stone tower which has been multiplied, joined together, and generally jumbled in with several other architectural facets to produce a type of storybook castle. Queen Victoria and her husband, Prince Albert, thought Balmoral was beautiful —and in its sylvan setting, it really is.

Old houses? If you want to see a really old one which has had people living in it continuously since the tenth century, go to Innerleithen in Peeblesshire and visit Traquair House. Kings and princes have lived there, and the place is peopled with ghosts from the past. (It also brews its own ale, which may be the reason the ghosts hang around.)

The little town of Culross on the north shore of the River Forth near Kincardine is a delight to visitors interested in sixteenth- and seventeenth-century architecture. The little town was built by Sir George Bruce, who must have realized the economic advantages of having the king and his court installed at the palace, while he established a good trade in salt and coal.

Modern architecture of the sixties and seventies can be seen at Stirling University, built on the old Airthrey Estate near Bridge of Allan. And somehow, in spite of its modernity, it blends quite well with the surrounding green countryside.

All over Scotland the general feeling of its architecture is of something built to last. The stone is solid, the design rather severe, but the effect is of something eternal. Of course, there are modern homes now which will never endure the years with the same grace their grey stone predecessors have. And in the cities there are great high-flying

multiple dwelling units and faceless apartment buildings
set in parkland where flowers are not allowed to survive.
But in the villages and small towns and in the rural areas,
the grey stone is still there and should remain for more
generations to enjoy.

The fine arts do not have as venerable a tradition in
Scotland as architecture does. Painting played a very small
part in history before the eighteenth century. Obviously,
there were some painters, but they were few and, until
Allan Ramsay and Henry Raeburn, without international
stature. Gaels tend to express themselves in music and
stories rather than in painting. But both Ramsay and
Raeburn have left us outstanding portraits, which depict
the Scots of their day in a unique fashion—unique inasmuch
as any native can look at the portraits and exclaim, "What a
Scottish-looking face!" There's something about Raeburn's
rosy-cheeked, pleasant-faced, but strong women and his
rugged, not really handsome men that seems just right to
many Scots. Both Ramsay and Raeburn traveled in Europe
before settling down at home, and both studied in Rome.
Other Scottish painters have achieved fame within the
boundaries of their own country, but few beyond.

In 1826 the Royal Scottish Academy was founded and
became the main place to see the best paintings of the day.
When Impressionism took hold on the Continent, a group
grew up known as the Glasgow School, which combined
many of the new styles and specialized in rich colors and
design.

In 1897 an unusual Scot, Charles Rennie Mackintosh,
founded the Glasgow School of Art, the "advanced" design
of which caused a great furor in its day and was frowned
on by many.

Just before World War I a new Scottish painter, who
had studied in France and had been strongly influenced by

Cézanne, entered the art world. His name was S. J. Peploe, and he left several paintings that are considered to be worthy examples of contemporary art.

Today many artists are clinging to the past by pursuing the old crafts—weaving, silversmithing, and carving. Scotland's silver was well known in the eighteenth century for its simple lines and expert craftsmanship, and some of the finest Scottish silversmiths enriched the culture of the New World when they immigrated to North America. Today Celtic jewelry is finding a place with tourists and Scots alike, and, although much of it is ghastly imitation, the best is beautiful.

Sculpture has always played a minor role in Scotland, although some of its castles have striking examples of human figures in stone, mostly created by masons imported from France. At the Field of Bannockburn is an outstanding equestrian statue of King Robert the Bruce in bronze—created, however, by a gentleman of Anglo-Saxon heritage from over the border.

Most countries, when they want to preserve historic buildings and battlefields, call on the government for help. But not so in Scotland. Back in 1931 a group of Scots got together and formed the National Trust for Scotland, an independent organization which over the years has become keeper and preserver of more than 5 million pounds' worth of property.

The trust is not government supported. Its funds come from people who are concerned about the preservation of Scotland's heritage, and since the Scots are proud of that heritage, the trust has flourished.

Legally supported by several acts of parliament, the National Trust takes care of approximately eighty separate properties ranging from cottages and castles to islands, mountains, and a large part of several small towns,

Being landlord to properties of historic value is not an

easy job. Who can put money value on palaces which have housed ancient royalty or on small simple cottages that were the homes of such great men as Robert Burns, James Barrie, and Thomas Carlyle? In its present position, the National Trust not only preserves but also restores many buildings and sites which natives and visitors enjoy the year round. It also makes recommendations about future preservation and is dependent on people with property of historic value to bequeath that property to the trust for the enjoyment of future generations.

The trust believes that the houses of Scotland's past also have a place in its future, and to illustrate this they offer to help buyers restore old buildings in their original style. This has led to some delightful areas in towns like Dysart, St. Monance, and East Kilbride, all of which have restored cottages and houses that are presently inhabited.

The small town of Culross in Kincardineshire has a large group of sixteenth- and seventeenth-century buildings which have been restored by the trust and which lend the town a unique appearance. Visitors are enchanted by the grey stone and the crows' steps on the gables, and it's not hard to imagine that you're hearing the strains of a medieval lute or getting a glimpse of a velvet skirt disappearing round a corner.

Culzean Castle, where President Eisenhower had a permanent apartment made available to him, belongs to the National Trust. So do other such stately homes as Craigevar Castle of Aberdeenshire, built in 1626 in Scots Baronial style; Leith Hall; the House of Binns in West Lothian; and the Royal Palace of Falkland, where James V turned his head to the wall and whispered as he lay dying, "It cam' wi' a lass, it'll gang wi' a lass," when he heard of the birth of his daughter, Mary Queen of Scots.

The trust also cares for some of the most beautiful of

Scotland's gardens. Of these, the gardens of Inverewe in Wester Ross are among the best known. Warmed by the Gulf Stream, palms and other tropical plants grow in the same latitude as that of Siberia.

The wilds of Glencoe, with the mountains called the Five Sisters of Kintail in their midst, are also under the care of the trust—so that no one will ever "develop" their 14,200 acres. And the islands of St. Kilda and Fair Isle are also protected.

Perhaps some of the places that are even closer to the hearts of Scots everywhere are those commemorating either great deeds or great people. Such is the tragic moor of Culloden, graveyard of the cream of the Highlands in 1745, and visited still every year by more than a hundred thousand people. Culloden was the last battle fought on British soil and one of the bloodiest in the turbulent history of the island.

Centers in several different areas have been set up to display "History on the Spot," as the trust calls it. One of these centers is at Bannockburn in Stirlingshire, where King Robert the Bruce defeated a large force of English soldiers in 1314 and established an independent place for his nation.

The National Trust for Scotland is just that—a trust *for* the people, caring for the history and beauty of the country. More than sixty-four thousand members yearly send money in support of the good work. With membership (as low as $7.50 annually), comes free access to all properties of the trust in Scotland, plus those in England, Wales, and Northern Ireland. Buying a membership is more than just a wise investment for tourists. It is a contribution to history itself.

For further information, contact the Secretary, National Trust for Scotland, 5 Charlotte Square, Edinburgh EH24DU.

Grouse shooting on the moors of Inverness-shire.

CHAPTER 7

HUNTIN', SHOOTIN', FISHIN' AND MORE

IT HAS BEEN SAID, "Scratch a Scotsman and you'll find a golfer." That is not strictly true, although there are lots of Scots who love the game and play regularly at much lower cost than the average American.

Scotland is the home of golf—and don't believe anyone who says that the Scots got it from the Dutch. The game was undoubtedly invented by two Scotsmen one day several hundred years ago when they were out walking in that cold East Fife wind and thought they would warm themselves up by hitting pebbles with a couple of sticks. "I'll hit it farther than you, Mac," one of them said. And so the drive was born.

People come to the town of Saint Andrews from all over the world, just to be able to say they played in the "home of golf." The Royal and Ancient Golf Club is truly both ancient and royal, since many kings have played there—most of them not very well—and is open to anyone who has the cash (about three dollars a round) and the patience. Saint Andrews has several other courses open too, so don't feel put out if the line is long at the R and A. In fact, every town in Scotland, almost without exception, has its own golf course—even little places of fewer than a thousand people may sport a nine-hole course, and you may find their uphill-downdale topography a challenge to your game.

There are 375 different courses listed by the Scottish

Tourist Board, and you can take your choice. Most of them have no introduction requirements, many are public, and several private clubs happily open their doors to visiting golfers. There are a few sticky ones who like you to be a "member of own club" and a few that even demand a certificate of handicap, but there are many more where you can walk right in and play.

After Saint Andrews probably the best-known course to Americans is Turnberry, where President Eisenhower often played. And, of course, Gleneagles, which has become almost exclusively the center for wealthy tourists. It is certainly beautiful and, if you can afford it, shouldn't be missed.

A large segment of the Scottish population is crazy about a sport quite different from golf—soccer, or "fitba' " if you speak the lingo. Every Saturday afternoon thousands pile into buses, trains, and cars to support their local clubs, which might be Dundee United, Rangers, Celtic, Hearts, Hibs, or any one of a hundred others. The most remarkable offshoot of the soccer teams throughout Britain has been the Football Pools, and Scots are every bit as enthusiastic about "ra pools" as anyone else in the island. For the small sum of fifty cents, if you guess all the winning teams, you can be almost a millionaire overnight.

Rugby football, or "rugger," is not played by as many people in Scotland as it is in England. There are, however, many high schools where it is the main sport, and the games are popular with a certain group. In the Borders in particular rugby is a sport regarded with a passion not often seen among canny Scots, and sporting feuds are common among towns and villages.

Swimming is a sport in which the Scots excel, although the climate confines competition swimming largely to indoor pools. Towns like Motherwell have produced many swimming champions from their public pools, known to locals as "the baths." Since Scotland has so many lochs, swimming in summer is always popular, and you haven't lived until you thrust your feet into an icy Highland lochan. That'll get your circulation going—or maybe cut it off!

The lochs in certain areas are also much in use for sailing, and there are many places which provide yachting instruction during vacations. You can sail on the beautiful Holy Loch in the Firth of Clyde, canoe on Loch Morlich, or water-ski on Loch Earn or a dozen other lochs, where the surrounding countryside is like living poetry.

One company advertising its sailing vacations baldly states, "You can call it a holiday if you like . . . but be prepared to get blisters, frightened and tired," in crewing Britain's largest sailing vessel, a three-masted topgallant schooner called the *Captain Scott*. The company runs four-week adventure cruises, for boys aged sixteen to twenty-one, all year round. Fees vary from two hundred fifty to three hundred dollars for the four weeks, and when ashore the boys are expected to do some hardy hill-trekking in the Highlands.

Enjoying the countryside is something Scots do without thinking. They are great walkers and hikers, and the roads in summer are traveled by a lot of young people from home and abroad. Those visitors who want to get farther from the beaten path may try pony-trekking and find some delightful out-of-the-way places on horseback. The Highlands and Islands offer varied opportunities for pony-trekking at spots like Strachur in Argyll, Killiecrankie in Perthsire, and Dunvegan in the Isle of Skye, where the mountain panorama often includes deer and eagles.

Until a few years ago, winter sports in Scotland included little other than skating, sledding, and an interesting pastime called curling. Curling used to be purely an outdoor sport, calling for a frozen loch or pond where large smooth granite stones were hurled down a runway and men ran around with brooms shouting, "Soop! Soop!" (Experts will undoubtedly call this an oversimplified version, but childhood impressions die hard.) Anyway, either the winters grew warmer and the solidly frozen lochs became scarce, or people decided they preferred artificial ice in the comfort of an air-controlled indoor rink. The fact that curling is now more of an indoor than an outdoor sport in Scotland is a shame, because few scenes can be more picturesque than a group of bemuffled players on a pine-fringed loch thickening the frosty air with their breath.

Along with indoor rinks Scotland has acquired the new sport of skiing. With the installation of several ski centers during more recent years, skiing has become very popular with the Scots. There are at least fourteen different ski schools, (many boasting a "Continental Ski Instructor") which tutor beginners and others from mid-December until May, and there are artificial slopes in Edinburgh, Glasgow, Dundee, Polmont, and Aberdeen open all year round.

The three most developed ski centers are in the mountainous areas of Cairngorm in Inverness-shire, Glenshee in Perthshire, and Glencoe, the infamous Glen of Weeping where a sept (a branch of a clan) of the MacDonalds were wiped out by their enemies the Campbells almost three hundred years ago. Now the glen echoes in winter to the swish of skis and the shouts of skiers.

An organization which has done a great deal for sports encouragement in Scotland is undoubtedly the Scottish Youth Hostels Association, with their national office in Stirling. For a very small fee, young people from the age of twelve upwards to "twenty-one plus" can participate in all kinds of year-round activities. Originally, the hostels provided only overnight accommodation for travelers. You brought your own sleeping bag to a hostel bunk in a dormitory, cooked your own food in a communal kitchen, and joined in group singing if you cared to. Now the association offers a variety of what they call "Breakaway Holidays" involving climbing, canoeing, pony trekking, sailing, walking, fishing, trail-riding and skiing. For example, a one-week skiing "breakaway" at Loch Morlich, including accommodation, instruction, meals, travel to hostel from main town, and snow slopes costs approximately eighty-five dollars for a "twenty-one plus."

The youth hostels have opened up Scotland, and the rest of Europe too, to a large segment of the younger population who would otherwise have found traveling either too expensive or too difficult. Now, as members of a hostel association, they can travel throughout Britain and the Continent, staying very inexpensively at hostels and mixing with young people from all over the world. In Scotland, as in other countries, many of the hostels were originally beautiful stately homes that have been given over to the YHA, and some are ancient castles, which may be drafty but are exciting to sleep in.

For people who prefer something even more energetic than hiking and hostelling, Scotland can offer some excellent climbing and rock-scrambling. The Scottish Mountaineering Club in Edinburgh has information on all peaks worthy of a climb, and these may range from small hills of a thousand feet or so up to the majestic Ben Nevis, 4,406 feet high and the highest point in the British Isles. The view from the top of eleven-hundred-foot Dumyat in the Hillfoots area is a panorama of valley, river, and grey stone villages that is the final benediction to a two-hour hike up springy turf.

In the Island of Skye stand the rugged Cuillin mountains, where you can enjoy the best rock-climbing in Britain. As you climb, you will understand the words of the old song,

" 'Tis the far Cuillin that is puttin' love on me."

The names of the Highland peaks are all Gaelic and fascinating to the Sassenach and foreigner. Buachaille Etive Mor (The Large Shepherd), which stands at the southern entrance to Glencoe, is the Scottish Matterhorn. Climbers find peaks like Suilven in the far northwest not so interesting to climb as the spectacular long ridges of Liathach, Beinn Eighe, and the crenellated An Teallach.

If climbing is too energetic for you, Scotland offers superb angling. Here are some of the most beautiful rock-strewn rivers in Europe, and the royal art of salmon fishing is open to all visitors. The Scottish Tourist Board invites even would-be fishermen to come and fish. Schools will teach you how to cast and bait and use rod, reels, and lines, and for about ten dollars you may rent any type of rod and reel you need for a week. There are special schools for boys (and it is to be hoped, girls) during school vacations, and the Board offers a complete guide, "Scotland for Fishing" from their Edinburgh office. Trout and salmon are the most popular fish in fresh waters, but sea-angling also yields fish like huge skate and halibut.

The king of game sports is deer-stalking and hunting for wild fowl. "Hunting" as a term is rarely used in Scotland except for deer. All gun activities are simply called shooting. You can shoot grouse, pheasant, blackcock, capercaillie (wild turkey), pigeon, wild duck, goose, snipe, rabbit, and hare in Scotland and, also, red deer. There are great areas of wood and moorland that abound in game, and accommodation of different kinds is available everywhere.

The average Scot is not a great hunter, although a fair percentage of the rural population enjoys its own type of hunting, more accurately known as poaching. There are still rabbit snares set in many country fences and hedges, and pheasant and salmon often find their way into cooking pots where they do not legally belong. Licenses are required to shoot game, and of course licenses are required just to own firearms. Gun licenses are almost invariably obtained. Game licenses not so invariably—one drawback may be that they cost about fifteen dollars per year. However, tourists may obtain "occasional" game licenses covering a fourteen-day period for under five dollars.

The season for stalking the red deer begins officially on July 1 and lasts until October 20, and deer stalking is confined to the Highlands with their vast stretches of moor and woodland. It is not an inexpensive sport. Visitors wishing to use the services of an experienced ghillie, or keeper, should be prepared to spend about three hundred and fifty to five hundred dollars for a week's hunting, a time in which several stags could be taken.

On August 12 Scots celebrate the "Glorious Twelfth," when the grouse shooting season opens. By then most of the birds are full-grown, and it is legal to shoot all but any remaining "cheepers" (small birds). Grouse shooting to many conjures up Victorian scenes of men in tweed knickerbockers (plus-fours to the initiated) and women in veiled hats sipping tea out of flasks behind shooting butts. In some places it's still like that—just put headscarves in place of veiled hats and add rifles in the ladies' hands.

Highlanders in particular like to boast that their particular corner of Scotland offers a wider variety of game and the very best sport to be had anywhere. There is a story about one Highlander who was asked by a visiting sportsman from the south if there were any centenarians on the island. Not wishing to let down the reputation of his local moors, he cautiously replied, "Weel now, I'm not chust too sure about that. But I did hear a story at the post office that the very last one was shot only yesterday."

What to do after an invigorating day climbing, skiing,

fishing, or shooting? For many, the answer lies in enjoying one of Scotland's most famous products, dubbed in Gaelic *usquebaugh,* "water of life." Someone has said that if the Irish invented whisky, the Scots were the first people to make it palatable. Although there are still some of us who continue to find it unpalatable, almost 200 million gallons of Scotch were distilled last year, and a large percentage went overseas to more than one hundred and seventy countries. You can drink Scotch in Ghana, Malawi, Greenland, Rumania, and even Sri Lanka (which imported 12,736 gallons in 1973, so if you ever get there, be sure to order a Scotch.)

The actual origins of whisky are, like Scotland's early history, not clearly defined. The Irish may have invented it and brought it over to Scotland with Columba, who undoubtedly used it as a medicinal aid. Where the Irish got it is a further mystery, but writer Douglas Young says that they picked it up in Greece during their early Celtic meanderings. Whatever, the first time whisky is mentioned in writing in Scotland is 1494, when the Scottish Exchaquer Rolls show an entry of "eight bolls of malt to Friar John Cor wherewith to make aquavitae."

The word *whisky* is a corruption of the Gaelic words for aquavitae, or water of life, *usquebaugh* or *usige beatha.* The main ingredient of whisky is barley, and if you have read some of Burns' poems, you will note his references to John Barleycorn, an affectionate nickname for whisky. Burns also says in "Tam o' Shanter"

> Wi' tippenny [ale] we fear nae evil,
> Wi' usquebaugh, we'll face the devil.

Whisky has several names in Scotland, and Scotch is possibly the least used. If a Scot goes into a pub and orders whisky, he or she says, "I'll have a half, please," and the bartender knows exactly what the half is meant to be. If you order "a half and a pint," you get a small glass of whisky and a pint of beer. If, as a tourist, you are invited to have "a wee dram," expect that dram to be Scotch.

There are two types of whisky—pure malt whisky made from malted barley only; and grain whisky made from malted barley plus unmalted barley and maize. The first type is made by the pot still process and the second by the patent still process.

To make pure malt whisky, distillers follow four stages: (1) malting, in which the barley is soaked, then spread out to germinate, and then dried in the malt kiln; (2) mashing, in which the dried malt is ground and mixed with hot water, thus forming a sugary liquid; (3) fermenting, in which yeast is added to convert the sugar into crude alcohol; and finally, (4) distilling, in which the liquid is heated to a vapor which rises up the still and passes into the cooling plant, where it condenses. Two distillations are necessary, and even with the second, there is waste at the beginning and the end.

The patent still process is a continuous one, and the spirit finally distilled is of higher strength.

Both pure malt and grain whiskies have to mature in casks of oak wood for long periods—up to fifteen years or longer for the malt in some cases. When matured, the whiskies are usually blended. This blending produces most of the big-name whiskies on today's world markets. Some Scottish distilleries retain a portion of their whisky to sell as pure, unblended malt whisky. Such are Glenlivet, Glenfiddich, Glenmorangie, and a few others—known to connoisseurs as gems for the palate. (But if you haven't drunk a pure malt whisky before and want to try its pale sparkle, be sure you're sitting down at the time. In fact, wear a hat to keep your scalp down.)

The art of whisky blending, like all successful arts, requires years of experience as well as pure ingredients. Most Scotch whisky sold in the United States (and Americans buy 40 percent of the export market) is the blended variety. The different flavors are the results of different combinations of spirits from different distilleries. Those flavors may be affected by the water, soil, and air in a district and, like people, their qualities have to mix well before a good blending is achieved. There are more than one hundred main brands of Scotch available in Britain and more than one hundred which are exported.

In spite of the high tax imposed on whisky in Britain, a great deal of it continues to be consumed. Statistics show that between 15 and 20 percent of total British consumption occurs in Scotland—a rather alarming fact, considering that Scotland's population is only one-tenth of the whole island's. Back in the eighteenth century, when Dr. Samuel Johnson and his trusty friend Boswell were making their grand tour of Scotland, Johnson remarked in his journal, "A man of the Hebrides as soon as he appears in the morning swallows a glass of whisky; yet they are not a drunken race."

This statement seems hard to justify in the light of other eighteenth century accounts that tell us that at the time there was one public house for every seventy people in Scotland!

Thomas Smollett, that anglicized Scotsman who wrote novels when hardly anyone else was writing them, said in *Humphrey Clinker,* "The Highlanders . . . regale themselves with whisky, a malt spirit . . . which they swallow in great quantities without any signs of inebriation; they are used to it from the cradle and find it an excellent preservative against winter cold."

Scotsmen are apparently still finding whisky an excellent preservative.

Before the eighteenth century those Scots who could afford to drink drank French wines and brandies. Claret in particular was popular in Scotland. But as the Highlanders, who had always been whisky drinkers, moved farther south and the society of the day slowly became integrated, more and more Lowlanders and English were introduced to whisky.

Athole brose is an old recipe in which whisky, cream, heather honey, and a little oatmeal are blended to form a drink which many still find delightful. "Hot toddy" is a popular remedy for all colds and bronchial complaints and is even given to children in Scotland. This is whisky diluted with hot water and flavored with lemon juice and sugar. Even teetotalers may occasionally deign to drink a hot toddy in the interests of "good health." And a little whisky rubbed on a baby's swollen gums is still recognized as soothing during teething troubles—although no one has ever decided whether it soothes the gums or the baby.

The popularity of whisky all over the world seems to be ever on the increase, judging by statistics issued by the Scotch Whisky Association in Edinburgh. Perhaps the most complimentary act is imitation, and now the Japanese are producing their own brand of Scotch. But they might save themselves the trouble. Scotch is *Scotch,* and to make it you need Scottish malt, Scottish water, and Scottish skill. Tourists are invited to call in at some of the many distilleries while they are visiting Scotland. William Grant's Glenfiddich distillery up in Dufftown near Elgin in the Highlands gives tours, and there are others closer to Prestwick Airport—for example, at Girvan and Ladyburn in Ayrshire, where visitors are welcome.

"Nessie's" peaceful home is really an inland sea of great depth.

CHAPTER 8

THE LOCH NESS MONSTER

ON A GREY DAY WITH a low cloud cover and a light rain falling, you may look down the long expanse of Loch Ness and see the still smoothness of its waters—and wonder, as thousands of others have done, just *what* is lurking in its depths.

The Loch Ness Monster, known to Scots in general as Nessie, and to locals around the loch as "the Beastie," has been the object of conversations around comfortable hearthsides for generations. The earliest mention in writing of the monster is in Adamnan's account of the life of Saint Columba. That worthy saint not only put the fear of death into the Picts, but according to his biographer, he also scared away "a certain water monster" and duly impressed some Pictish bystanders. Since Columba's day lots of other people have sworn they saw strange objects in Loch Ness and have been prepared to stand by their statements. Obviously, some of these people could have been mistaken— perhaps they saw a floating tree or shadows on the water. But could all of them have imagined things?

Since the "new" road was opened along the loch side in 1933, the last forty years or so have produced a remarkable number of interesting accounts.

In 1934 a London surgeon was visiting Loch Ness when he was surprised by a disturbance in the water about three hundred yards away from where he was standing. A small head with a very long neck rose out of the water and remained long enough for him to take two quick pictures with his camera.

Again in 1934, Alex Campbell, for forty years water bailiff on Loch Ness, saw a creature he described as about thirty feet long with a flat, reptile-type head, thick-looking skin, and a hump at the base of a long neck. He watched it for several minutes before two fishing skiffs disturbed it.

Author Virginia Woolf tells an interesting story about a vacation she took in the thirties at Loch Ness. A tragic accident happened to a woman who was not only drowned in the loch but also went down wearing thirty thousand pounds' worth of pearls. Divers sent down to recover the body and the pearls found neither. Instead, they came back with reports of a frightening black cave underwater, where the temperature was unusually warm. They were very afraid and refused to dive again.

A husband and wife driving from the village of Dores reported being astounded by a huge animal undulating across the new road in front of their car and disappearing into bushes by the lochside. When they got out of the car to investigate, the creature had disappeared into the loch.

Reports like these—although the latter is one of very few describing the creature on land—have continued to come in, and the general picture gathered over the years is as follows: Nessie is probably about thirty to fifty feet long with a ten-foot neck and a small, flat head. She (many prefer to think of her as feminine) has a long tail and a wide back with one or more humps and elephantlike skin. Some accounts say that her eyes are slits, like a reptile's; others say that she has two tiny protrusions like horns. She also has powerful flippers or paddles, can move extremely fast, has acute hearing, and is of a bashful disposition. She has been seen at all times of the year, appearing mostly in the early morning. But she also likes to come out to bask in the sunshine. She has been seen by farmers, fishermen, housewives, engineers, doctors, school children—you name it. She has been seen singly, in pairs, and in large groups, and the consensus is that the Loch Ness Monster is no myth. She is a fact. Indeed, she may be more than one fact. Nessie is probably only one of a group of creatures inhabiting Loch Ness, and various theories have been put forward to substantiate this.

How could a creature or creatures of such an alien type be living in a Scottish loch?

First of all, we must examine the loch, its background, and its physical makeup. Loch Ness is actually deeper than the oceans which surround the United Kingdom, and at one point near the ruins of Urquhart Castle the depth of the loch is twice the mean depth of the North Sea. Millions of years ago, when the ice from the Great Ice Age was melting and forming the lochs of Scotland and the fjords of Norway, Loch Ness was connected to the ocean. A huge fault line, known today as the Great Glen, cracked across the Highlands, forming a chain of lakes that was joined much later by modern Scots to form the Caledonian Canal system, which stretches from Inverness through Loch Ness, Oich, and Lochy down to Fort William. When Loch Ness flowed into the ocean, undoubtedly many fish and other creatures swam upstream and inland in search of food, and it is possible that certain species decided to remain in the upper areas of the loch system. Over thousands of years before people were around to build canals, banks of sand and silt formed at the mouths of these sea-lochs until gradually many became land-locked. Loch Ness became one of these inland seas. After Loch Lomond, which is twenty-six miles long, it is the largest loch in Scotland, and it contains more water than any other lake in Britain —263,000 million cubic feet of water. It is fed by eight rivers and sixty major streams, with dozens of other smaller streams running into it from the surrounding hills. The water maintains a deep water temperature of forty-two degrees Fahrenheit all year round. The loch is unpolluted but carries minute particles of peat which render visibility below the surface very poor. Divers who have gone into Loch Ness talk of a quiet darkness underwater, which is not only uncomfortable, but sinister.

There is a common saying, "Loch Ness never gives up her dead," and it is true that the bodies of people drowned in the loch are never found. Could it be there is something or some things down there which dispose of the bodies? Certainly the sides of the loch in many parts show steep rock walls dropping into the water, and divers have reported deep shelves beneath the surface.

What kind of creatures then could be inhabiting these surroundings?

There are several theories, each supported by different people, but the one which currently seems to have most support is the plesiosaur theory. A plesiosaur is a type of dinosaur believed to have been extinct for the past few million years. Yet consider the coelecanth, another prehistoric animal. Over the past thirty years people have caught almost thirty coelecanths in the South Atlantic, and before that time they were believed to have been extinct for 70 million years. Could this not also be true of the plesiosaurs? Skeletons of plesiosaurs have been found in other areas of Britain, and their resemblance to Nessie show that this theory is a strong possibility.

In order to maintain a species over a great length of time, biologists tell us, fourteen is probably the minimum number of individuals necessary, so this may mean that there are actually seven families of "Beasties" living in Loch Ness—

which would account for some differences in description also. Tim Dinsdale, who has spent a great deal of time and effort studying the situation, believes that at least one huge creature, the "bull of the herd," is probably considerably larger than some of the others.

If Nessie is not a plesiosaur, what is she?

F. W. Holiday, one of Loch Ness's many investigators, believes that she is a giant sea worm, an enormous invertebrate, and he entitled the book he wrote about her *The Great Orm of Loch Ness.*

Others say she is an unknown amphibian, a type of monstrous newt; or perhaps a long-necked seal-like mammal or a colossal eel. Certainly there are millions of eels in Loch Ness, and an eel expert says he thinks the loch is an eel-trap, into which migrating eels swim instead of returning to the open sea, as would be expected. So there is food for large creatures in the loch in great quantities.

With all this information available, what investigation has been carried out?

Back in 1933, when the new road caused a spate of sightings and "Loch Ness Monster Seen Again" was quite a common headline in the papers, lots of people rushed up to Scotland to see the new attraction. One of the people rushing north was Bertram Mills, who had the bright idea of putting Nessie into his circus. Unfortunately for him, his methods were not acceptable to the locals, who didn't like his idea of using dynamite to raise the monster. The law stepped in to protect "the contents of the loch"—a fact which sheds an interesting light on the lawyers of the day.

Any official investigations were put off by the hoax of a prankster who made giant hippo footprints on the loch shore and had everyone very excited until the trick was uncovered. So, very little was done, save by a few private individuals, until after World War II. Not that Nessie went into hiding. According to reports, she continued to pop up regularly and was seen by a variety of reputable people, including a man in 1943 who was watching for enemy bombers through his binoculars. He described an animal having a body about thirty feet long, a neck about five feet high raised out of the water, large eyes in a small head, and a fin-like thing on the back of the neck.

In 1957 an enterprising Scottish woman, Mrs. Whyte, whose husband was manager of the Caledonian Canal, put together accounts of all the encounters with Nessie she could find, talked with dozens of local people, and produced an interesting book called *More Than a Legend,* which inspired several other people to start investigations.

In 1960 Oxford and Cambridge universities sent thirty students who spent two months at the loch in bad weather, but came back with no conclusive reports. In 1962 a two-month long expedition worked with fifty-seven volunteers on hydrophones listening to underwater noises.

In October 1962 a film was taken of Nessie in action. It was shown to a group of four scientists, who stated there was definitely "some unidentified animate object in Loch Ness, which if it be a mammal, amphibian, reptile, fish or mollusc of any known order, is of such a size as to be worthy of careful scientific examination and identification."

In the early sixties the Loch Ness Investigation Bureau, a nonprofit operation, was set up and functioned for several years under the auspices of various enthusiasts.

In 1966 the Loch Ness Investigation Bureau was encouraged by an official report from the Joint Air Reconnaissance Centre of the Royal Air Force—that group of photographic experts who had worked overtime during World War II. After viewing Dinsdale's film of a large moving object in Loch Ness, they declared it to be "probably an animate object."

In 1968 and 1969 sonar equipment was moved in to the loch, and a couple of submarines sent down into the murky depths. The larger sub, *Pisces,* located ancient weapons on the floor, along with a wreck and lots of fish. And then—it located a large, moving object which eluded their sonar equipment.

In 1969 an Englishman, Frank Searle, decided to take up "Loch Ness watching" as a way of life. In six years he logged more than twenty thousand hours of watching, every day from dawn till dusk, and obtained twenty-three sightings of Nessie. His pictures are among the best that have been taken so far.

Expeditions by the Academy of Applied Science in 1970, 1972, and 1975 disclosed interesting findings through the use of sonar. It was ascertained that Loch Ness had a series of very deep channels in its floor, channels within which a very large fish or eel-eating creature would have no difficulty hiding.

The 1970 expedition detected very large moving objects in the loch with sonar, and the later expeditions also employed a camera-strobe light system to take pictures of whatever might happen by. On the night of August 8, 1972, the observers watched sonar traces that raised the hair on the back of their necks. Two large moving objects were very close, and the pictures taken that night were distinct enough to show a large flipper on one of the objects. The size of the flipper was calculated as being from four to six feet long.

The sonar-camera expeditions of 1975 yielded further pictures of large, cylindrical objects, and one picture gave an impression of the head of a large creature.

In 1976 there is talk of the Smithsonian Institution sending out a further investigative expedition.

Nessie, your days of seclusion may be numbered!

Shadows walk the halls of Glamis Castle where Macbeth murdered Duncan.

CHAPTER 9

GHOULIES AND GHOSTIES, FOLKLORE AND FANTASY

SCOTLAND IS VERY ACTIVE WITH ghoulies and ghosties and things that go bump in the night. Every county has a preponderance of castles and ancient houses, and almost every historical site boasts at least one ghost. There are ghostly sounds, smells, songs, and pipes, not to mention sundry Green Ladies, kilted warriors, and a few floating heads.

It has been said that places like Scotland and Ireland actually produce a ghost that is Celtic in type. Whether this is true or not, the ghosts of Scotland often have nationalistic qualities that set them aside from other run-of-the-mill ghosts. Where else would you be likely to see a kilted clansman hiding out on a twentieth-century moor? Where else could you claim that an invisible army led by a pipe band actually marched through your living room? One man said this happened in his old Highland residence.

Several families have ghosts that herald special events or disasters due to occur to that family. The Campbells of Inverary are forewarned of the death of a chieftain by a ghostly galley sailing down the loch. The Earls of Strathmore, who live in Glamis Castle where the Dowager Queen Elizabeth was brought up and where Princess Margaret was born, have a long, haunting history of mysterious evils still supposed to linger in the castle. According to legends, a monster of vampire type is born periodically into the Strathmore family. The monster may live for hundreds of years and is kept locked up in a room with a hidden door. During fairly modern remodeling activities at the castle, rumor has it that some workmen found the bricked-up door and were induced to emigrate rather than divulge the awful secret. There are certainly some spirits walking in Glamis, for several shadowy figures have been seen by reliable sources. One long-dead ancestor who tied himself to the devil is said to play an everlasting game of cards with Auld Nick and some of his cronies. Another Glamis ghost is the restless spirit of Janet Douglas wandering in the Clock Tower. She was burned at the stake in the sixteenth century for alleged witchcraft—she was accused of plotting to kill the bride of James VI as she was arriving by sea from Denmark.

Whatever happens at Glamis happens in a suitably gloomy setting, for the castle is very old. Some of it was built in the eleventh century, and its history was morbid from the first— it is supposedly the castle in which Macbeth murdered Duncan.

At Hermitage Castle in Roxburghshire, the ghost of a warlock haunts his old stamping grounds. Lord Soulis was a horrible creature who used to kidnap local children to use in his heinous experiments. The villagers finally got wise to his activities and threw him into a barrel of molten lead. He and his helpmeet, Red Cap, still wander around Hermitage.

Over at Drumlanrig in Wigtownshire, Lady Anne Douglas's ghost has created a stir on several occasions by appearing with her head in her hand, and up at Dunphail Castle in Nairnshire there are a few severed heads that float around unsupported. Not far away from Dunphail, at Rait Castle, the ghost of a young girl who has no hands and wears a blood-stained dress has appeared several times. She was a daughter of the Cummings (or Comyns) and in love with a Mackintosh youth at a time when the Cummings and Mackintoshes were feuding. The Cummings invited the Mackintoshes to dine, intending to murder them, but the Mackintoshes arrived armed. The chief of the Cummings believed that the girl had betrayed her own family by warning her lover. Accordingly, the chief himself, who was also the girl's father, cut off her hands, and she leaped to her death from the tower.

Female ghosts are quite common, and there are at least five "Green Ladies" who appear at different locations. Fyvie Castle, Aberdeenshire, has one, and Ballindalloch Castle another. The lady at Crathes Castle picks up a ghostly baby from the hearth. Ashintully Castle, known as the most haunted house in Scotland, has Green Jean, who comes back to remind people that she was murdered for her money by her uncle. Huntingtower Castle in Angus has a ghostly lady wearing a dress with green sleeves. And in the same county, at Newton Castle, Green Lady Jean walks every Halloween at midnight after her gravestone has turned around three times.

Green is the favorite ghostly color, but there is also a Pink Lady at Stirling Castle. She walks across the courtyard to the area where, several hundred years ago, the ladies used to watch their lords jousting. She has been seen several times in recent years by soldiers living in the castle and is said to be wearing a pink dress surrounded by a pink light.

One famous Scottish woman, Mary, Queen of Scots, haunts Borthwick Castle in southeastern Scotland. She came there as a bride of the Earl of Bothwell after the mysterious murder of her husband Darnley. Later she left disguised as a page. Her ghost at Borthwick appears as a boylike page.

Next to Mary, Queen of Scots, the most famous historical figure in Scotland must be Bonnie Prince Charlie, another unfortunate Stewart. His ghost haunts Culloden House near

Inverness, where his last battle in 1746 saw the end of his army. Culloden Moor itself is a sad, grey place that still shelters memories of the bloody battle. People visiting there are often impressed by the gloom of the area, and strange sounds are sometimes heard in the night. An army has also been seen in the sky above the moor.

There are at least three other battles that are periodically reenacted. One of them is an ancient battle against invading Norsemen that is fought every May Day just after dawn on a moor in Inverness-shire. Another is an eighteenth-century battle at Glenshiel, and a third a clan fight between the MacDonalds and MacLeods back in 1395, which two students saw happen all over again in 1956. The bloody, two-hundred-year-old Battle of Killiecrankie recurred in the nineteenth century, according to a startled observer who suddenly found himself surrounded by wild-eyed, fighting clansmen.

Not all encounters with Scottish spirits are frightening, however. If you walk by a cairn near Lochalsh, you may hear the most beautiful music in the world. At Balcomie Castle in Crail you may hear the whistling ghost boy who was hanged for whistling against orders. If you're out in the western islands you may hear a mermaid singing to the sea. In the islands there are many ghost stories of friendly spirits who warn fisherfolk of impending danger and show them where the best fish can be caught, and there are some mysterious moving lights that no one can explain.

If you are sports-minded, visit Dalarossie Kirkyard in Nairnshire on a year when Christmas Day falls on a Sunday. On that day in the early morning, two ghostly teams play a silent game of shinty, an early form of hockey. And if you like mountain climbing, you may meet the Grey Man at the top of Ben Macdhui, a peak in the Cairngorms. He has been seen by many climbers. Also, if you're female and happen to visit Kylesku Hotel in Ross and Cromarty, be very careful when you go to the ladies room, where you may be surprised by a male ghost who lowers himself down through a trapdoor in the roof.

There is a phantom piper at Culzean Castle, a bothy (a farm outbuilding) haunted by a vampire in Kincardineshire, and indelible bloodstains at Buckholm Tower in Galashiels, where ghostly hounds bay in the distance. Even Edinburgh boasts a coach driven by the devil racing through town, bearing his disciple and seventeenth-century warlock, Major Weir.

Out in the countryside, you might meet a phantom on the road if you're walking or cycling home after dark. If you're near Castle Douglas, Kirkudbrightshire, look out for a friendly black dog which may keep you company for a while. But if you try to pat it, your hand will go right through its head. And if you're driving on the Stow road in Midlothian, about twenty miles from Edinburgh, be careful not to follow a phantom truck which may be nasty enough to lead you right into a wall. Several accidents like this have been reported.

One of Scotland's best-known ghost stories concerns the Campbells, the ruling clan of Argyllshire. Inverawe House is haunted by the ghost of one Duncan Campbell, whose cousin Donald was murdered by an Appin Stewart. Duncan, who had unwittingly given hospitality to Donald's murderer, was visited three nights in a row by his cousin's ghost, imploring him to murder the Stewart in revenge. Duncan would not betray the trust of his guest, and Donald finally left after saying, "Meet me at Ticonderoga." The name Ticonderoga meant nothing to Duncan at the time, but three years later in 1758 he sailed for North America with his regiment, the Black Watch, to fight in the Seven Years War. He was killed at Ford Ticonderoga, and his spirit has returned to haunt the house of his birth, Inverawe.

Duncan Campbell and his ghostly counterparts in castle, moor, and stately home are waiting for you to pay them a call.

But ghoulies and ghosties are not the only mysterious inhabitants of Scotland. Many Scottish children grow up with the belief that if there are no fairies actually living at the bottom of *their* gardens, there are certainly fairies living in other people's gardens.

When you live in a rural area, it's not difficult to believe in the "wee people." They may be inside a bluebell, under a stone, or just around the next corner. Both the mist and the fine rain that so often shroud the Scottish countryside are conducive to nurturing a belief in the supernatural, for they lend mystery to the most ordinary places.

For example, there is a forty-ton boulder in Glen Nevis, called Samuel's Stone after a chief of the MacSorlies. Although Samuel's Stone looks perfectly ordinary, it turns around all by itself, three times a year. If you happen to be there at the time, the stone will answer any questions you might have.

There are many such beliefs still alive today, although many of the more primitive superstitions have died away, helped by the new magic, television.

Since the weather plays a vital part in Scotland (and is hard to ignore because it's often not very good) there are many beliefs still held about it. For example,

> Evening red and morning grey
> Is a sure sign of a beautiful day.
> But evening grey and morning red
> Put on your hat or you'll wet your head.

Or,

Ne'er cast a clout
Till May be out
[that is, don't take off any winter woolies before May 31]

Or,

St. Swithun's Day if thou be fair
For forty days 'twill rain nae mare.
St. Swithun's Day if foul and wet
Half the winter's tae come yet.

Don't kill a spider or you'll bring the rain on, and don't put up an umbrella indoors or lay it on a bed for the same reason. (People must be doing this a lot in Scotland.)

Then there are certain times of the year or month or week when certain things are best attended to. You cut peats (chunks of peat are used for fuel in some parts of Scotland) when the moon is waning, and you dig ditches at the same time. But you cut hair when the moon is waxing, and don't ever keep a lock of it because "he who keeps hair, keeps care."

When the moon is new, you must bow to it three times and turn over the money in your pockets. And it's bad luck if you see that new moon through glass—although perhaps spectacles are allowed.

Do your washing on Mondays, as it's only "dirty folk" who wash on Saturdays.

Sneezing and cutting nails are also allied to days of the week, and you should choose your day carefully:

Sneeze on Monday, sneeze for danger;
Sneeze on Tuesday, kiss a stranger;
Sneeze on Wednesday, sneeze for a letter;
Sneeze on Thursday, something better;
Sneeze on Friday, sneeze for sorrow;
Sneeze on Saturday, see your sweetheart tomorrow.

As for your finger and toenails,

> Cut them on Monday, cut them for health;
> Cut them on Tuesday, cut them for wealth;
> Cut them on Wednesday, cut them for news;
> Cut them on Thursday, a new pair of shoes;
> Cut them on Friday, cut them for woe;
> Cut them on Saturday, somewhere to go.

But *never, never* cut them on Sunday.

Not only must you never cut nails on Sunday, you must never whistle then either, because that "makes the angels cry." And if you start something new on a Saturday night, such as sewing or knitting, it will not be finished for seven Saturdays. If you keep something for seven years, however, you'll be sure to find a use for it.

In the spring, go out and catch the first bee of the season and put it inside your coin-purse if you want to be sure you have money for the rest of the year. Perhaps the saying "He's got a bee in his bonnet" originated with a Scot who was insuring his brains for the year.

In Scotland, as in many other places, when salt is spilled you throw a little over your left shoulder to save your luck. Don't walk under a ladder over there either, but a black cat crossing your path is very *lucky,* not unlucky. White heather is rare and, therefore, lucky. Lucky trees are the oak, holly, hazel, and apple. A bird flying into your house is a very bad omen, and if you put a new pair of shoes on the table (even while inside the box) your luck will turn bad. And if you put on a garment inside out, don't change it or your luck will change with it. So if you ever meet a Scotsman with his kilt round the wrong way, you'll know why.

Count to ten if you have to go back for something you've forgotten, and if you're outdoors without a watch, consult a fairy clock. That's a seeded dandelion which you blow upon, counting one hour for every group of fluffy seeds that flies away.

Fairy clocks are just part of the whole folk culture of the Wee People, or the Daoine Sith as they are called in Gaelic. These are the Men of Peace, said by some to be fallen angels, and are better avoided. Legend says that back in the eighteenth century a young shepherd boy and his sister up in the wilds of Inverness-shire saw a long line of tiny shaggy horses bearing tiny riders in tartan jackets with long grey cloaks and red caps. The boy asked,

"What are ye, little mannie?"

And one answered;

"Not of the race of Adam; the People of Peace shall never more be seen in Scotland."

Still, they seem to be around in some places, for we hear of them often. There are Fairy Bridges, Fairy Knowes, Fairy Rings, and so forth, all over Scotland. In the Highlands ancient mounds are known as *shians,* or "fairy hills."

Fairy rings are dark-colored rings of grass found occasionally in fields or on hillsides. Perhaps they lead to that great Tir-Nan-Og, which is Fairyland, or the Land of Heart's Desire and Eternal Youth.

A traditional rhyme says,

> He wha' tills [ploughs over] the fairy green
> Nae luck again shall hae.
> An' he wha' spills [breaks] the fairies' ring
> Betide him want and wae [woe].
>
> But wha' gaes by the fairy ring
> Nae dule nor pine [sorrow] shall see;
> An' he wha' cleans the fairy ring [weeds it?]
> An easy daith shall dee.

Brownies are the fairies who care for cattle, and in the Highlands they are called *gruagachs.* Farmers' wives used to leave saucers of milk out for them at night. The MacLeods of Gesto were lucky enough to have a herd of white fairy cattle of their own, stories say.

The Kelpie is a fairy you must beware of. He is a water horse who lures people into his loch or pool in order to devour them. The problem with him is that he can turn himself into a handsome young man and once you touch him, you can never let go.

Beware also that the fairies do not take your new baby and exchange it for one of their own, or you will end up with a "changeling" who will give you a bad time.

In the old days there were many who believed in the "evil eye," and of course there were cures to counteract it. If you were sure a witch had put a spell on your cows and their milk turned thin and scarce, then you put a sprig of rowan berries from the ash tree at the door of the byre. And "silvered water" was also a sure cure for the effects of the evil eye. Silvered water is from a stream over which both the dead and the living have passed (usually a stream flowing under a bridge on the way to a cemetery) and into which a silver coin has been dropped. Silver has apparently always had strong powers against evil—witness the silver stake through the heart of a vampire.

Scotland never went in much for vampires, but the country certainly had more than its share of witches and used a lot of wood burning them up. The last witch was burned at Dornoch in the north in 1722, and she was at the end of a long line. Just to show how democratic they were, the Scots did not confine their witch trials to the lower classes. When James VI was awaiting the arrival of his bride from Denmark, a group of women was accused of raising storms at sea. One of the women was the daughter of a senator from the College of Justice, a young mother of three. She was further accused of framing a wax picture of the king and was burned at the stake. Her estate was confiscated by the crown, and one wonders if James could have had his eye on it anyway.

On a road near Forres in northeastern Scotland, there is a boulder with an iron bar attached where a witch was executed, and there must have been scores of magic spells chanted since the days of Macbeth's three hags on the heath.

One popular spell used to get rid of rats and mice was written on a scrap of paper and placed on the ground for the vermin to read, a practice which should convince you of Scotland's superior education system.

> Ratton and moose
> Awa' frae the hoose,
> Awa' ower tae the mill
> An' there tak' yer fill!

Spells lead us into home remedies, and there are plenty of these too. The old folk culture advises the following:

Ribwort poultices to "draw" a sore

Buckbean for the colic

Nettles for nosebleeds and headaches

Foxgloves to bring on sleep after a fever

Butter as an antiseptic

Deer's grease as a bone rub

Dulse, that panacea from the ocean, for skin diseases and headaches and constipation

For consumptive diseases, a special formula was required, since the cure lay in transferring the disease elsewhere. Nail parings of the patient were tied up in a piece of his clothing, waved three times around his head and then buried in a place unknown.

To cure a case of epilepsy, a black rooster had to be buried alive at the spot where the first epileptic attack took place. Fortunately, most home cures have been improved upon, and we now have the National Health Service, which is more clinical, if less picturesque.

There are some wells in Scotland today, the water of which local people say has healing properties. And many twentieth-century Scots not only believe in the "second sight" but also have had some experience of it. The second sight is traditionally gifted to the seventh daughter of the seventh daughter, so there are presumably not too many exponents around. Whatever, it is a gift more to be feared than cherished, as those who have it can foretell the future, which often involves tragedy. For example, to see someone surrounded by a grey mist (the "winding sheet") means that person will soon die.

There are still speywives around, who for some silver (or maybe paper in these days of high wages) will read your palm or your tealeaves. The tinkers who still wander on Scottish moors and roads will sometimes offer to read your palm, although their numbers are diminishing rapidly with the onrush of modern society.

By far the greatest prophet of the future in Scotland's history was a man whose predictions are still, according to some, being fulfilled. Kenneth Mackenzie was a Highlander from the Black Isle near Inverness, born at the beginning of the seventeenth century and known familiarly as the Brahan Seer. (The name Brahan came from the farm where he worked as a laborer.) He acquired his powers as a young man, and legend says that his mother was responsible for his receiving the gift.

One summer evening as she was tending her cattle on a ridge overlooking a burial ground, she saw all the graves open and the dead rising and dispersing in all directions. About an hour later they all returned, but she noticed one grave still empty. Being braver than the average person, she ran down to the burial ground and placed her distaff across the mouth of the grave, because she had heard that this would halt any spirit. In a few moments she saw a tall fair lady rushing through the air.

"Lift thy distaff from off my grave and let me enter my dwelling of the dead," said the fair one.

"I shall do so," answered Kenneth's mother, "when you tell me what kept you so long after the others."

"My journey was much longer than theirs," the ghost replied. "I had to go all the way to Norway. I am a daughter of the King of Norway. I was drowned while bathing in that country, but my body was found and buried here. In remembrance of me, I will leave you a powerful secret for your son Kenneth. Go to that lake over there and you will find a small round blue stone. With that stone Kenneth shall know the future."

During the years that followed, Kenneth Mackenzie became famous in the land, and he was invited to gatherings of the wealthy all over the Highlands. At his final gathering, however, he was foolhardy enough to tell the Countess of Seaforth (head of the Clan Mackenzie) why her husband was taking such a long time to return from Paris. Whereupon the angry lady ordered the seer to be pushed into a burning tar barrel and exterminated.

Several of the Brahan Seer's prophecies have been fulfilled. Some of them involved death and destruction; for example, he forecast the bloody battle of Culloden more than one hundred years before it happened. The most detailed prophecy concerned the demise of the House of Seaforth, which Kenneth decried to the countess just before he died. He forecast that the last chief of Seaforth would be deaf and dumb, that his four sons would die before him, and that his estate would be inherited by a "white-hooded lassie from the east" who would kill her own sister. Less than two hundred years later, after several generations of Mackenzies had watched their family progress with bated breath, all the aforementioned came to pass. Lord Seaforth, who had become deaf as a young boy after a bout with scarlet fever, lost the last of his four sons and became totally inarticulate thereafter. He never spoke during the latter part of his life. He was succeeded on his death in 1815 by his eldest daughter, a recent widow just returned from India in white widow's weeds ("white-hooded lassie from the east"). Some years later this heiress was driving her younger sister in a carriage when the ponies bolted and both ladies were thrown to the ground. The sister was fatally injured. The estates of the Mackenzies were gradually disposed of over the years, until now the name of Seaforth is part of the past.

Several of the Brahan Seer's other prophecies have not yet come to pass and, hopefully, not all of them will. There is one in particular which many are discussing eagerly today. Kenneth forecast that one day "black rains" would cover Scotland and that "the people will return and take undisturbed possession of the lands of their ancestors." Some believe the "black rains" might indeed be the oil recently discovered off Scottish shores. In which case, will all the Scots abroad soon be rushing home to the land of their fathers? Get your teacup out fast and read the leaves for the answer.

A statue of the "immortal Rabbie" in Dumfriesshire where the young poet died. The wild flowers in his hand are a gentle, telling touch.

Chapter 10

NOVELISTS AND POETS

ASK AN OUTSIDER TO NAME a Scottish writer, and the most likely answer will be Robert Burns, the "immortal Rabbie." Although there have been many notable Scottish writers, Burns probably enjoys the widest international reputation. Not many people know that he wrote the words to "Auld Lang Syne," the song sung around the world every New Year's Eve.

Burns was an unusual sort of chap, a couthy farmer who lived during the "Silver Renaissance" of the eighteenth century. To begin with, he had very simple origins and less than three years of formal education, although he had a good knowledge of literature, counting, and languages. His poetry shows an understanding of both people and nature that seems far beyond the erudite. He was a son of the soil, born to a small farming couple in Ayrshire in 1759 and fated to spend most of his days trying to maintain life just above the subsistence level. With his first success as a writer, he went to Edinburgh, where he was fêted by the society of his day. But apparently that society did not make a great impression on him, as he later wrote, "The rank is but the guinea's stamp;/The man's the gowd for a' that." In other words, titles and money do not necessarily indicate a good person.

Burns was a man of many parts—one part giving a very good imitation of Casanova. He fairly peopled the country-

side with small Burnses, mostly without benefit of matri-
mony, and as a youth spent some of his time sitting on the
"cutty stool" in church on the Sabbath, being berated for
his sins by the minister and kirk session. He was also fond
of the bottle, and, like the characters in his poem "Tam o'
Shanter," he loved to "sit bousing at the nappy,/An' gettin'
fou' and unco happy." It was one night after a few hours
at the public house with his cronies that he staggered home-
wards, fell asleep outside in the cold, caught pneumonia,
and died prematurely at the age of thirty-seven. He had
made a great contribution to his country's literature in
poetry and song, mostly in the vernacular, but sometimes in
English, and he died before his work was finished. His songs
include one of the most beautiful love songs ever written—
"O, my luve is like a red, red rose,/That's newly sprung in
June./O, my luve is like the melodie,/That's sweetly played
in tune." He was, of course, an expert on love songs, because
he was constantly in love, but he convinces us of his depth
of feelings as an honest, warm and earthy soul.

His poems of nature, "To a Mouse" and "To a Mountain
Daisy," for example, show how close he was to growing and
living things. He saw them every day as he worked in the
fields, and he understood their condition as well as his own.

Every Scottish school boy and girl reads and learns portions of "Tam o' Shanter," one of Burns's most famous poems.
It is a vividly descriptive poem about the drunken ride of
Tam on his good mare Maggie past the old haunted Kirk at
Alloway at midnight, where all manner of ghastly creatures
are cavorting about to the music of bagpipes played by Old
Nick himself. All is well until Tam, attracted by one young
witch wearing nothing but a short shift (a cutty sark),
shouts out encouragement to her, and "in an instant all was
dark." Well, Tam had scarcely rallied his horse, "when out
the hellish legion sallied." And what a chase they gave him!

Tam knew he had to cross the bridge to save his life, because the devilish company could not cross running water, so on he pelted hell for leather, with Maggie sweating and panting, and with a great final effort he reached the bridge and safety —although Maggie lost her tail in the pursuit. The telling of this tale, the pace of the words, the movement of the chase—Burns conveys it all with such verve that if the poem is read aloud, the reader is left almost breathless at the end.

Rabbie Burns has retained his magic for two hundred years—possibly because he was a universal man, the kind of man lots of men would like to be. He was a "man's man" whom women adored, a creative genius who became a national hero, and his early death served only to enhance the romance of his life.

After Burns, the next Scottish writer many think of is Robert Louis Stevenson. Stevenson was born in Edinburgh in 1850, into a middle-class home. He was the only son of a civil engineer and the grandson of a famous lighthouse builder. He was a sickly child and fought ill-health most of his life. But when he was a child, his condition offered him the opportunity to do a lot of reading, observing, and thinking, and the charming poetry he wrote for children when he was an adult reflects the kind of delightful childhood he must have had. Here's "The Lamplighter":

> My tea is nearly ready and the sun has left the sky;
> It's time to take the window to see Leerie going by;
> For every night at teatime and before you take your
> seat
> With lantern and with ladder he comes posting up the
> street.
>
> Now Tom would be a driver and Maria go to sea,
> And my papa's a banker and as rich as he can be;

But I, when I am stronger and can choose what I'm
    to do,
O Leerie, I'll go round at night and light the lamps
    with you!

For we are very lucky with a lamp before the door,
And Leerie stops to light it as he lights so many more;
And O! before you hurry by with ladder and with light;
O Leerie, see a little child and nod to him tonight!

Stevenson's book *Treasure Island* was in its day a departure for children's literature, telling as it did a swashbuckling tale in an adult way, sparing few grisly details but carrying the adventure through to the end. The tale is still good today. Similarly his stories *Kidnapped* and *Catriona* are exciting, and his classic, *Dr. Jekyll and Mr. Hyde* holds, among tales of horror, a place of honor that will never be changed.

Stevenson has a small place in American history also, because he went to the United States, crossed to California, and spent some time in Monterey. He married a Mrs. Osbourne, an American, and they moved to the South Seas. Stevenson died in Samoa, the island he loved, at the age of forty-four. He wrote his own epitaph:

Under the wide and starry sky,
Dig the grave and let me lie.
Glad did I live and gladly die,
And I laid me down with a will.

This be the verse you grave for me:
Here he lies where he longed to be;
Home is the sailor, home from the sea,
And the hunter home from hill.

A sentimental bunch, the Scots, and they have been unashamedly encouraged to be so by another great writer, Sir Walter Scott. Scott was a lawyer turned author who often wrote thirty pages a day. He was the inventor of the historical novel as such, and the first writer to give a fair account of both sides of the Scottish-English conflict. He wrote almost twenty long novels (really long!) and several long narrative poems, and his work was popular all over Europe. To him Scotland owes the glamorization of the Jacobite Rebellions and much of the restoration of Highland regalia to public life. Scott was largely responsible for arranging the visit of King George IV to Edinburgh in 1822—the first visit of any Hanoverian monarch to Scotland—and spectators were delighted to see both Scott and His Royal Highness in full Highland dress. In fact, this set off quite a fashion, and members of the Royal family visiting Scotland today often show up in the kilt.

Today's readers find Scott's novels pretty hard going. Who wants to spend time wading through four or five chapters before the plot thickens? But if you have the fortitude, the novels are worth reading. Goethe, probably Scott's greatest contemporary acquaintance, on hearing that Scott had completed his lengthy *Life of Buonaparte,* wrote, "What could now be more delightful to me, than leisurely and calmly to sit down and listen to the discourse of such a man, while clearly, truly and with all the skill of a great artist, he recalls to me the incidents on which through life I have meditated, and the influence of which is still daily in operation?"

And to every Scotsman overseas, Sir Walter's lines have special meaning:

> Breathes there the man, with soul so dead,
> Who never to himself hath said,
> This is my own, my native land!
> Whose heart hath ne'er within him burn'd,
> As home his footsteps he hath turn'd
> From wandering on a foreign strand!

Scotland's early poets, from the sixteenth century, are rarely read now, save by scholars who know the names of Dunbar, Henryson, and Gawin Douglas. Sir David Lindsay's great play, *The Three Estates,* was first performed in Linlithgow in 1540 and since revived at the modern Edinburgh Festival. King James I of Scotland was the royal writer of an epic, *The Kingis Quair* (The King's Book), and in the sixteenth and seventeenth centuries King James VI also published several works including one book on demonology. It may have been easier to get something published if you were a king. . . .

The eighteenth century produced a shoal of writers and poets in Scotland, apart from Burns. One of the fathers of the English novel was actually a Scotsman, Tobias Smollett, a doctor, who wrote about the dirt and disease of his society. John Galt was another novelist (1779-1739), who wrote a book about the effects of the Industrial Revolution on a small parish in Ayrshire, *Annals of the Parish.*

Then there was the young boy-poet Robert Fergusson, of whom some said he would have been greater than Burns had he lived past the age of twenty-four. And James Hogg, the "Ettrick Shepherd" of the Borders.

The year before Burns was born, Allan Ramsay died in Edinburgh, where he had been not only a bookseller, publisher, and librarian, but also an author of work like *The Gentle Shepherd, Tea Table Miscellany,* and *The Evergreen.*

James Boswell, best remembered for the journals of his life with the great Dr. Samuel Johnson, was a Scot from near Edinburgh.

Thomas Carlyle, the great Victorian historian, was a Scot. His ponderous works remain too ponderous for most of us today, but those of his compatriot, the eighteenth-century philosopher, David Hume, are still studied in universities around the world.

More recently, Scotland's literary offspring have included two men from Orkney, Eric Linklater and poet Edwin Muir. And where would American actress Mary Martin have been without *Peter Pan,* created by Scotsman James Barrie? James Bridie, a Glasgow dramatist, wrote mainly for the Scottish audience, but his play *The Anatomist* received approval from all over. Some novelists include S. R. Crockett, Neil Munro, D. K. Broster, Nigel Tranter, James Barke, Compton Mackenzie, Mary Stewart, Helen Mackinnes—and one favorite from the thirties, John Buchan of the famous *Thirty-Nine Steps.* Some of Scotland's greatest poets write only in Gaelic, and as such cannot be wholly appreciated by many. One of them, Sorley McLean, has been called the Verlaine of Scotland.

All of these writers wrote from their own personal experience of life in Scotland, as it was in the past and is now. They are all still being read somewhere by people in Scotland and around the world.

The poem of another great poet, Hugh MacDiarmid, epitomizes the feelings of most of them:

> The rose of all the world is not for me.
> I want for my part, the little white rose of Scotland
> That smells sharp and sweet
> And breaks the heart.

Sir Alexander Fleming, a Nobel prize winner for his discovery of penicillin, is one of a long line of distinguished Scots in medicine.

CHAPTER 11

DOCTORS, SCIENTISTS, AND INVENTORS

"May no English nobleman venture out of the world
without a Scottish physician, as I am sure there is none
who ventures in."   (—William Hunter [1718-1783])

IF YOU ARE EVER IN THE hospital for an operation, take a
moment, as you are wheeled into the operating room, to
thank the Scots pioneers who helped make your surgery not
only possible but also comfortable.

John Hunter (1728-1793) of Glasgow was the first
surgeon in Britain to practice something more refined than
butchery. He worked at Saint George's Hospital in London
at a time when very little was known about the workings of
the human body and surgery was a hit or miss affair—
mostly miss. His own work in dissection, examining dead
bodies to understand how they had functioned, made him
the founder of pathological anatomy. In the course of his
studies, Hunter also devised a method of tying badly swollen
arteries—a revolutionary process for his time. He died while
experimenting, rather less successfully, with veneral disease,
having injected himself with both gonnorrhea and syphilis
simultaneously, believing they were the same germ.

John's older brother, William, also a doctor, was a pioneer
in the field of obstetrics. He wrote a tome called *The
Anatomy of the Gravid Uterus* when virtually nothing was
known about prenatal matters—and when the subject was
certainly never discussed outside medical circles.

Both John and William were inveterate collectors of bits and pieces of the human body, and they were the founders of the Hunterian Collection at the University of Glasgow, one of the finest museums of anatomy in the world.

Writer Donald Cowie states that although "Hunter taught surgeons of the world how and where to cut, . . . he was quite unable to stop his victims from shouting out loud." As you are dropping into blessed oblivion on the operating table, you can thank Edinburgh's obstetric surgeon, James Young Simpson (1811-1870), who experimented successfully with chloroform and first introduced it to society in 1847. Without the arrival of anaesthetics, it is doubtful that surgery would ever have gained much in popularity.

Then, as you find yourself in the recovery room, give another thought to Joseph Lister (1827-1912), professor of surgery at Glasgow University in 1860. Lister observed that every second surgery patient died, even after what might reasonably be termed successful surgery. They were, in fact, dying from infection. So Lister initiated a top-priority scrub process, whereby all instruments, dressings, equipment, and personnel involved in the hospital were subject to lavish scrubbings with a carbolic acid solution. It worked. (Now you know why the brand name Listerine has such a positive approach.) Lister went on to become Lord Lister and was the first medical man to sit in the House of Lords.

These four men of medicine, therefore, made contributions not only to Scotland, but also to the world at large. Other Scottish doctors of note include Robert Philip (1857-1939), tuberculosis expert; Ronald Ross (1857-1932), who worked in tropical diseases (he verified the part mosquitoes play in spreading malaria); and John James Rickard Macleod, who was born in 1876 in the ancient town of Dunkeld and went on to become a leader in the field of diabetes research, heading the group which discovered insulin.

The name of another Scot, Alexander Fleming (1881-1955), is permanently linked with penicillin. Alec Fleming was born in the Scottish Lowlands and spent his boyhood on a farm. When his family moved to London, he attended the medical school at Saint Mary's Hospital, and it was in a small laboratory there that he carried out his painstaking experiments which in the late thirties led to the use of penicillin as a combatant of disease.

Medicine is not the only science that owes a great deal to the Scots. As far back as 1614, mathematician John Napier of Merchiston, who was educated at the University of Saint Andrews and enjoyed living the life of a country gentleman, published a book about his discovery of a whole new concept—logarithms. He has been favorably compared with both Galileo and Danish astronomer Tycho Brahe. And the impact of his book rates second only to that of Newton's *Principia*.

The science of geology grew in stature through the contributions of James Hutton and Hugh Miller. Hutton (1726-1797) wrote a widely influential book called *Theory of the Earth,* thereby earning the title of "father of modern geology." Hugh Miller, born in a thatched cottage in Cromarty in 1802, started life as a stone mason before turning to geology and writing. Of course, it was helpful that the Scottish Highlands, whose ancient and fascinating rock formations have found a place in all geology textbooks, were on their doorsteps.

Another science founder was Edward Forbes (1815-1854), whose study and descriptions of life zones in the sea led to what we now know as oceanography.

Probably one of the most vital scientific contributions made to the world by Scots has been in the field of physics. James Clerk Maxwell (1831-1879) of Edinburgh unlocked secrets that led to tremendous progress in the areas of optics, color, electricity, and magnetism. His work at Cambridge provided the foundation for the later development of radio, television, and radar, for future study of X rays and ultraviolet rays. He also formulated the kinetic theory of gases and studied color blindness. The books written by this versatile scientist, *Theory of Heat* and *Electricity and Magnetism* became basic texts for all future physicists.

Scottish men of science have been noted for their practicality. It's fine to have theories, but practical application is needed. James Young (1811-1883) was a Glasgow chemist (and friend of David Livingstone) whose experiments led to the mass production of paraffin oil (kerosene) for domestic use. William Murdock lighted his own home and office by coal gas in 1792, and in 1802 had the pleasure of seeing the first streetlights go on in London's Soho district—which had long been in need of illumination.

James Dewar (1842-1923) was the inventor of the vacuum flask and also of something less benign—cordite explosive. William Ramsay (1852-1916) discovered helium and neon. William Thomson, Lord Kelvin, (1824-1907) improved the compass, invented the tidal gauge, and stated the second law of thermodynamics. Robert Sibbald (1641-1722) was a great naturalist, the founder of Edinburgh's Medical School, and in his spare time the designer of the Botanical Gardens.

Among Scots scientists was a man called Charles Macintosh (1766-1843), one Charles amidst a bevy of Jameses, Williams, and Roberts. (Very unimaginative with the names, the Scots.) Charles was a chemist who experimented with rubber solution and came up with—you guessed it—a waterproof coat, subsequently called the macintosh. Macintosh and John L. McAdam, therefore, donated their names to the world. McAdam gave his in the form of a road-laying process which ever after was known as the macadamized surface—pulverized stones sprinkled with water and pressed down flat.

Scottish children used to read the story of James Watt (1736-1819), who as a child watched the lid of his mother's tea kettle rise and fall as it sat boiling upon the hearth. This was supposed to have made him rush out and invent the steam engine—something he did do in time. Another Scot, called James Nasmyth (1808-1890), put Watt's work to further good use by inventing the steam hammer in 1839. At the age of seventeen Nasmyth had built and operated a small steam engine in his home. Also working with steam was William Symington (1763-1831), who powered the *Charlotte Dundas* under steam five years before Fulton's first ship appeared in the United States.

A blacksmith's son, Kirkpatrick Macmillan, made the first bicycle in 1839, and a few years later a veterinary surgeon called John Dunlop discovered that by tying a length of rubber hose on to the wheel rim of a bicycle, you could get a much more comfortable ride. He and a friend joined together to found the Dunlop Rubber Company.

The Stevenson family—Robert Louis's father and grandfather—provided the country with a series of excellent lighthouses during the nineteenth century, and an engineer called Thomas Telford (1757-1834) built 920 miles of highways. Telford was the son of a Border shepherd who earned for himself the facetious title of "Colossus of Roads." He built bridges also, including the first suspension bridge in Britain, spanning the Menai Straits, and was largely responsible for the building of the Caledonian Canal.

In 1888 a man was born in the small seaside town of Helensburgh, a man who in his lifetime was the inventor of something which today forms such an important part of the American way of life. John Logie Baird (1888-1946) projected images on a screen to an amazed audience back in the twenties and became the inventor of black and white television. Unfortunately for him, the British did not clearly recognize the fantastic potential of his discovery, which was taken over by the Germans in 1929 and patented. In 1941, when the British and Germans were at war, Baird unlocked the secret of color television also, but he died in 1946 without much recognition in his own land.

Probably the best known inventor of all to come out of Scotland was Alexander Graham Bell (1847-1922), inventor of the telephone. Bell was born and educated in Edinburgh and emigrated to Canada at the age of twenty-three.

Altogether that's a formidable list of useful people for a country the size of Scotland. There are more besides—and there will still be more to come.

The military Tattoo on the castle esplanade is a nighttime highlight of the yearly Edinburgh Festival.

CHAPTER 12

MUSIC AND THEATER

THE FACT MUST BE FACED that not everyone appreciates the music of the bagpipes. To the uninitiated, the sound they make approaches the wailing of banshees. But a good piper playing outdoors makes music to gladden the heart of every Gael and stir any drop of Scots blood that might flow through the veins of a "furriner."

The early history of the pipes is as vague as the beginnings of whisky. The ancient Greeks are known to have had a bag which they squeezed, together with reeds through which they blew, and the Irish also had a similar instrument. Long ago the harp used to call men to war, and the Highland *clarsach* is recognized as an ancient instrument. But it was not until the early days of the sixteenth century that every chief had his own piper and played for battle assembly and during battle.

The MacCrimmons, hereditary pipers to the MacLeods, are known as the greatest pipers in all Scotland, and to them goes credit for evolving a special form of pipe music known as Seol Mòr (Big Music), or Piobaireachd (anglicized to pibroch), which is the classical music of the pipes. The MacCrimmons' school on the Isle of Skye has become world famous. Strict rules are applied to the composition of the pibroch, and the music is complicated and stylized. People who understand it have compared it with the sonata, and even those who do not are nevertheless fascinated by competitions featuring pipe-playing Highlanders trying to outdo each other in musical skill.

Pipe bands consist of pipers and drummers only, with a gentleman called the Pipe Major up in front flourishing a grand staff. Traditionally, since these bands became popular with the military, the men wear Highland dress complete with busbies, which are tall bearskin hats. All the famous clan regiments had their own pipe bands—the Seaforths (Mackenzies), the Cameron Highlanders, the Gordon Highlanders (Marquis of Huntly), the Argylls (the Campbells), and the Sutherlands (who formed the famous Thin Red Line at the Battle of Balaclava in the Crimean War). No self-respecting Scottish regiment moves far without its pipers, and the pipes have sounded on the African veldt, in the Himalayas, and above the mud of Flanders.

The Scottish police force were the forerunners of police pipe bands which have also sprung up all over the world. Indeed, Scots abroad make grand "bobbies." The Edinburgh Festival for 1975 invited the Pipes and Drums of the Australian Police to take part in the Tattoo on the esplanade of Edinburgh Castle.

You may ask, "What is a Tattoo?"

The military Tattoo, which has become so popular as part of the annual Edinburgh Festival, is what the French call a *son et lumière* ("sound and light") performance. With the great stone castle lit up behind them, massed bands parade on the esplanade every night during the festival, making a striking spectacle guaranteed to bring a lump to the throat. Tickets are always hard to obtain unless bought early, because local Scots who may not care so much for chamber music or opera will turn up in large numbers for the pipes.

Other music that is popular with Scots is country dance music, and for a long time the name of Jimmy Shand was magic in the Lowlands. If Jimmy Shand and his band were playing at the dance, there was sure to be standing room only. His type of band relied mainly on piano and accordian, and the accordian in particular has always sounded good on Scots dance floors.

The fiddle has also had its day. The greatest fiddler of the eighteenth and nineteenth centuries was a gentleman called Neil Gow from Dunkeld. He was not only a great performer but also a composer of country music. His son Nathaniel followed in his footsteps.

In the area surrounding the River Spey in northeastern Scotland, an area known as Strathspey (the valley of the Spey) a new dance form originated, and by the end of the eighteenth century people were tapping their feet to it even south of the border. The rhythm of the Strathspey is slower than the reel rhythm of other dances. It is a deliberate and stately step still popular with dancers.

When Bonnie Prince Charlie was holding court in Edinburgh in 1745, he and his companions danced "Highland reels" at the Palace of Holyrood. And when he took flight through the heather, trying to elude the Redcoats, it is said that he danced reels to keep up his spirits and those of his companions.

The origin of solo dances like the Highland Fling is obscure, but undoubtedly the Scots have been dancing for hundreds of years, because with music like theirs how could they keep their feet still?

The sword dance, danced over crossed swords, is fascinating to watch—especially at the end when the music gets very fast, since the trick is not to touch a sword with the feet but to dance only in the spaces between. The best dancers can do it without looking.

Both men and women dance solo and group Highland dances, and the proper footwear is a soft leather heel-less shoe that ties up the leg. Toes are pointed and arches stretched, and if you haven't done it for a while, expect cramped feet until you get back in the habit.

At dances today—and the Scots are addicted to the custom of dinner-dancing which the big hotels like to encourage—there will always be an assortment of dances. Regular ballroom dancing is mixed with rock, and then someone will shout, "Let's have an Eightsome!" and groups will take the floor for an Eightsome Reel, which is great sport. But if you're short of breath or get dizzy going round in circles, don't join in! In the towns there are still dance halls where ballroom dancing continues in spite of rock and discothèques. And in a Glasgow dance hall you may still hear a fellow casually ask a girl, "Are ye gaun roon?" which to the uninformed means, "May I have this dance?"

Along with instrumental music and dancing, all Scots are brought up with songs. At almost every party someone will be invited to "Give us a song!" Anyone who has ever been out pub-crawling with a group of Scots knows that the evening could not end without songs of one kind or another (often another).

In the old days there were songs for every occasion, and the singing of them helped the task at hand. There were reaping, rowing, sowing, fishing, and weaving songs. In the Highlands, of course, they were all in Gaelic. It is part of Scotland's tragedy that only a small segment of its population knows Gaelic, and the others are therefore excluded from the beautiful and bountiful tradition of Highland folk songs. The songs lose much in the translation, although the airs are both sweet and melancholy.

In 1891 a society was formed to preserve the traditions of the Gael in literature and music, and this society, An Comunn Gaidhealach, has done a job worthy of praise. Every year it sponsors a gathering known as the Mod which is attended by Gaelic speakers from all over the world, and there you will hear the finest music and songs of the Highland Scot. This is real mood music, and many of the singers seem to have stepped right out of ancient times.

Yet the Lowlands have their own songs too, and they are very lovely. Rabbie Burns wrote words to many old tunes, and Scottish children grow up with "Ye Banks and Braes," "My Love is like a Red, Red Rose," and "Green Grow the Rushes-o," while other songs like "Loch Lomond" and "Auld Lang Syne" are sung by millions overseas.

Bothy ballads are a distinctive song form available to folk song lovers. They are the songs of the farmhands who in the old days slept in an outbuilding (bothy) of the farmhouse where they worked. The songs are earthy and full of humor and pathos.

Many of the folk songs are about local occupations. "The Wee Cupar o' Fife" is about a barrelmaker who has problems with a snobbish wife, and "Caller Herrin' " is the song of the fishermen's wives as they sell the fresh fish but anguish over the well-being of their husbands out at sea. Other songs may be about the loss of a loved one, like "Annie Laurie," or about days gone by, like "The Auld Hoose." Perhaps the saddest is the song of the exile, epitomized in the anonymous lines of a Canadian-Scot,

> From the lone shieling of the misty island
> Mountains divide us, and the waste of seas.
> Yet still the blood is strong, the heart is Highland
> And we in dreams behold the Hebrides.

The Edinburgh Festival for almost thirty years has brought together some of the world's best musicians, dancers, and actors, providing for three weeks annually a glittering burst of stars. Thousands of tourists invade the capital, Princes Street is a constant throng, and you can hear every accent you ever thought of. The famous among Scotland's own are

put on view—the Scottish National Orchestra, the BBC
Scottish Symphony Orchestra, and the Scottish Opera Company, as well as Scottish choral groups, and chamber music
quartets. The Royal Ballet from London has some Scottish
members and is also present at the festival.

Some history books say that the restrictions of the Reformation made vital changes in the way of life in Scotland
and that rigid Presbyterianism cut out much of the pleasure.
Yet, the songs, music, and dance of the country do not seem
to have suffered at all and are still lending a unique charm
to its people.

Here are the words to a few of Scotland's best-loved songs:

Loch Lomond

By yon bonnie banks, and by yon bonnie braes
Where the sun shines bright on Loch Lomond.
Where me and my true love were ever wont to gae
On the bonnie, bonnie banks of Loch Lomond.
O, you'll tak' the high road and I'll tak' the low road
And I'll be in Scotland afore ye
But me and my true love will never meet again
On the bonnie, bonnie banks o' Loch Lomond.

Comin' thro' the Rye

Gin a body meet a body
Comin' thro' the rye;
Gin a body kiss a body
Need a body cry?
Ilka lassie has her laddie
Nane, they say, hae I
Yet a' the lads they smile at me
When comin' thro' the rye.

Auld Lang Syne

Should auld acquaintance be forgot,
And never brought to min'?
Should auld acquantance be forgot,
And auld lang syne?
For auld lang syne, my dear,
For auld lang syne,
We'll tak a cup o' kindness yet
For auld lang syne.

The Wee Cooper o' Fife

There was a wee cooper wha lived in Fife
Nickety nackety noo, noo, noo
And he has gotten a gentle wife
Hey, Willy Wallacky, hoo John Dougal
Alane, qho' Rushity, roue, roue, roue.

The Bonnie Brier Bush

There grows a bonnie brier bush in our kailyard
And white are the blossoms on't in our kailyard;
Like wee bit white cockades for our loyal Hieland lads
And the lassies lo'e the bonnie bush in our kailyard.

Ca' the Ewes to the Knowes

Ca' the ewes to the knowes
Ca' them whaur the heather grows,
Ca' them whaur the burnie rows,
My bonnie dearie.
Hark, the mavis evenin' sang
Soundin' Cluden's woods amang,
Then a fauldin' let us gang,
My bonnie dearie.

Nae Luck aboot the Hoose

And are ye sure the news is true?
And are ye sure he's weel?
Is this a time to talk o' wark?
Ye jades, fling by your wheel!
Is this a time to think o' wark
When Colin's at the door?
Gie me my cloak, I'll to the quay
And see him come ashore.
For there's nae luck aboot the hoose
There's nae luck at a'
There's little pleasure in the hoose
When oor gude man's awa'.

My Love is like a Red, Red Rose

O, my luve is like a red, red rose,
That's newly sprung in June.
O, my luve is like the melodie,
That's sweetly played in tune.
As fair art thou, my bonnie lass,
So deep in luve am I,
And I will luve thee still, my dear,
Till a' the seas gang dry.

O' a' the airts

O' a' the airts the wind can blaw
I dearly lo'e the west
For there the bonnie lassie lives
The lassie I lo'e best;
Tho' wild woods grow and rivers flow
Wi' monie a hill between
Baith day and nicht my fancy's flicht
Is ever wi' my Jean!

Caller Herrin'

Wha'll buy caller herrin?
They're bonnie fish and halesome farin';
Wha'll buy caller herrin', new drawn frae the Forth.
When ye were sleepin' on your pillows
Dreamt ye aught o' our puir fellows,
Darkling as they fac'd the billows
A' to fill our woven willows?
Wha'll buy caller herrin',
They're no' brought here without brave darin'
Wives and mithers maist despairin'
Ca' them lives o' men.

Ye Banks and Braes

Ye banks and braes o' bonnie Doon,
How can ye bloom sae fresh and fair?
How can ye chaunt, ye little birds
And I sae weary fu' o' care?
You'll break my heart, ye warbling birds
That wanton thro' the flowery thorn
Ye mind me o' departed joys
Departed never to return.
Aft hae I roved by bonnie Doon
Tae see the rose and woodbine twine
And ilka bird sang o' his love
As fondly sae did I o' mine
Wi' lichtsome heart I stretched my hand
And pu'd a rosebud from the tree
But my fause lover stole the rose
And left, and left the thorn wi' me.

A Man's a Man for A' That

Is there, for honest poverty,
That hings his head an' a' that?

The coward slave, we pass him by,
We daur be poor for a' that!
For a' that, an' a' that,
Our toils obscure, an' a' that;
The rank is but the guinea's stamp;
The man's the gowd for a' that.

Growing up in a small town in Scotland isn't exactly a cosmopolitan experience. But it does have its advantages. You can play tennis in summer, badminton in winter, golf all the year round—*and* you can join the local drama club. For a group that's supposed to be dour and phlegmatic, the Scots are very fond of the theater—perhaps because they can get rid of some of their own inhibitions by watching uninhibited antics onstage.

There are several distinct types of Scottish theater, all offering something of value. Humor can be bawdy and unsubtle in some Scots plays, but there is a quieter, wry form that often appears and makes for good folk theater.

Since the Scottish Community Drama Association introduced its first festival in 1927, amateur theater has flourished, and one-act plays in "Lallans" (Lowland vernacular) are still popular. A night at the local church hall during the association's drama festival can be a joy for a native Scot and a study in exasperation for someone who does not speak the language.

Variety shows were a popular theater form for many years also, but there is no doubt that the advent of television —which brings performers into the home nightly—can offer more in the way of entertainment today. But many remember the old days with fondness. One of the greatest artists of all time was Sir Harry Lauder, who could hold an audience quite easily for several hours by singing comic and sentimental songs and telling folksy stories. Sir Harry's theme song, "Keep Right on to the End of the Road," hid his own personal grief, for his only son was killed in World War I.

The Scots have always loved a singer, and if he wears a kilt and sings the "auld Scots sangs" like Kenneth McKellar and Andy Stewart, then so much the better. And sometimes a night at the theater is improved by a "guid greet" (a good cry).

One of the most popular forms of theater must surely be pantomime, or the "panto." What we think of as pantomime, gestures and facial expressions conveying a situation, is not what the British mean by pantomime, and the English are as addicted to panto as the Scots—or almost.

A Scottish pantomime is a form of musical comedy with certain very strict rules. The story is usually a free version of a nursery rhyme or a fairy tale, interspersed with the popular songs of the time and lots of slapstick. The Principal Boy (hero) of the cast is *always* played by a shapely young woman in tights, and the Dame (the comedy butt) is always played by a man, generally the star comedian. Some of the best known Scots comics like Will Fyfe, Tommy Lorne, Harry Gordon, Stanley Baxter, and Rikki Fulton have been hilariously cast in pantomime. Some of the best-known companies, like the King's Theatre in Edinburgh and the Perth Repertory Theatre, present special pantomimes each year, the favorite season being Christmas.

For Scottish children Christmas vacation would be incomplete without a visit to the nearest pantomime, where they can join in the popular choruses, sigh over the beauty of the heroine, and boo the Ugly Sisters or the Wicked Uncle.

Looking now at straight, professional theater, overseas visitors may be surprised to find how well-provided Scotland is with theatrical talent. For a small country it has a remarkable number of theatrical companies in business for all or part of every year.

In Saint Andrews back in 1933 a small theater company was formed in a four-hundred-year-old converted cowshed. The theater was named "The Byre." The stalls where the cows had been became the auditorium, and the feeding loft above was turned into dressing rooms and wardrobe for an energetic cast of professionals. Today's Byre Theatre is on a new site just thirty yards from the original theater. The new Byre, which seats 145 people, was built with monies raised by grants from Fife County Council and the Scottish Arts Council and with subscriptions from many local people as well as from famous personalities like Bob Hope and Bing Crosby. Between April and December, for the modest price of eighty to ninety pence (under two dollars), you can see a company of twelve actors present plays like *The Day after the Fair, Equus,* or *Peer Gynt*—or perhaps an original Scottish play by Alexander Peterson, the Byre's director.

If you leave Saint Andrews and go on to Dundee, you can attend theater in an old church on Lochee Road, where the local repertory company has been performing since 1963—the year its theater burned down. Owing to shortage of funds (a common complaint) the players have had to cut their season to nine months instead of twelve in Dundee, but audiences are good and Dundee Repertory's reputation continues to be excellent. The Rep. has a touring company which takes theater into small towns and villages, presenting plays like a musical version of Shakespeare's *As You Like It, Hedda Gabler,* and Molière's *Le Malade Imaginaire.* Dundee Rep. also has a small group playing in schools, presenting documentary plays written by their director, David Milne.

Perth Repertory Theatre, which opened in 1935, has the highest theater-going audience per head of population of any theater in Scotland, playing to more than three hundred people every night during the season. (Bear in mind that

Perth is a town of perhaps fifty thousand people.) Perth
Rep. opens and closes its season with a musical like *Cabaret*
or *Cowardy Custard,* and in the weeks between it presents
classic comedies and dramas, including at least one work by
Shakespeare. The top price for the best seats in the house is
one pound (roughly, two dollars).

For years the beautiful town of Pitlochry in Perthshire
has presented a festival of plays each summer, plays which
have attracted visitors from all over the country. Another
innovation of recent years has been theater and supper
served together in Kinross and enjoyed in a mediaeval setting. This last is known as Ledlanet Nights.

Scotland's two largest cities, Glasgow and Edinburgh, have
active theater-going citizens, who are judged to be among
the most discriminating in the United Kingdom. The famous
French company, Comédie-Française, used to come to
Glasgow every year and present plays in French—plays
that were well attended. Glasgow's old King's Theatre was
always the trial ground for new plays destined for London's
West End, but now that has gone, pulled down to make way
for "city improvements."

The Citizens' Theatre is located in the Gorbals district of
Glasgow, a neighborhood which was a slum back in the
thirties and forties and is still none too salubrious. The
theater was built in 1870, and the plays of James Bridie,
Scots doctor turned dramatist, were all presented there. In
1945 this historic theater changed its name from the Princess to the Citizens'. It has been a leader in presenting new
plays by native Scots and has produced a series of fine
actors, including Duncan Macrae and Lennox Milne.

Forty miles east of Glasgow lies the capital city of Edinburgh, and, as in every other area, there is intercity rivalry
in the theater. Edinburgh boasts that it has a touch of
"class" that Glasgow lacks, but Glasgow folk say "pride

and poverty." Glasgow people are very friendly and feel Edinburgh folk are just a little snooty. In fact they also say that Edinburgh is "East windy, West Endy"—and you can feel that snell east wind on winter nights as you come out of the theater. Even at the end of summer, if you go for the Festival, which is always the last week of August and the first two of September, be sure to take a warm coat.

During the festival there is a great selection of theater, from lavish productions in the majestic Assembly Hall to small "fringe" presentations in informal theaters. The Fringe program, originally on the edge of the Festival or just outside, has become almost as popular as the festival itself and presents a variety of theater, dance, and music.

Edinburgh's two largest theaters, the King's and the Royal Lyceum, are busy both during the Festival and during the rest of the year. The Lyceum has an offshoot known as the Young Lyceum now in premises of their own on Cambridge Street, where they have presented plays like *They Shoot Horses, Don't They?* as well as original musicals. Shaw and Eugene O'Neill continue to be popular with audiences at the Royal Lyceum, and original Scots plays are also presented. The King's Theatre enjoys touring plays such as *Night Must Fall* and takes time out for ballet also.

A delightfully unusual idea in theater was born over twelve years ago in Edinburgh with the advent of the Traverse Theatre Club in the Grassmarket. This small theater, which seats only one hundred people, is open to members for the sum of five pounds or approximately ten dollars per year and carries with it associate membership to several other small theaters in London. There is a restaurant and bar for members and guests, and during the year there are frequent late shows at 10:30 P.M., so that you may dine first and be entertained afterwards. Plays at the Traverse are often experimental or avant-garde, and many are original productions or premieres of foreign plays. If you are visiting Edinburgh for a brief time only, temporary day memberships are available for a dollar—even less for students.

Traveling players in Elizabethan days were very popular, and people in outlying areas delighted in having the theater brought to their own front doors.

Barrie and Marianne Hesketh of the Mull Little Theatre, located on the Isle of Mull off the coast of Argyllshire, are continuing in the tradition that if the people can't come to the theater, then the theater must come to them. For the past ten years these two professionals have presented "small plays," that is, plays with small casts, and have also adapted large cast plays for successful productions. With their son as stage manager, the Heskeths tour all over the country at the invitation of any group or person who will pay their modest fee. A real Elizabethan touch is their request for either "hospitality for the night" or subsistence expenses to cover accommodation and meals. Another interesting addition to the Little Theatre's program is a twice-weekly luncheon presentation of slides and commentary on places they have visited, all enjoyed along with a cup of Marianne's homemade tomato soup and a salad roll. In one season between January and April, Mull Little Theatre may play in as many as sixty theaters all over the country.

The Heskeths receive a supplementary grant from the Scottish Arts Council, an organization that recognizes the importance of maintaining high-quality theater.

All together the theatrical picture in Scotland is a varied one, and the quality is generally excellent. Certainly, some famous plays are derived from the Scottish heritage—plays like Shakespeare's *Macbeth,* Schiller's *Maria Stuart,* and Barrie's *Peter Pan*—to name a few.

And don't be fooled into thinking the Scots are all dour. Put them on a stage and see how they loosen up!

Beautiful Loch Rannoth in the Grampian Mountains offers a woodland idyll.

CHAPTER 13

A GREEN GARDEN: FLORA AND FAUNA

WHEN THE ROMANS PUSHED UP INTO Scotland more than two thousand years ago, their way was impeded not only by painted men but also by thick forests. The dense woods of Caledonia were a good reason to stay south of the border. But several hundred years of burning and chopping and plundering by generations of careless people, both native and foreign-born, dispensed with most of the vast forest land, and today there are only a few remnants of the ancient Wood of Caledon.

Trees of ancient times were oak, holly, hazel, alder, pine, birch, and aspen. The larches that are prevalent on the Scots landscape today were introduced to the country in the eighteenth century in the form of three lone trees from the Austrian Tyrol. Since then they have been crossbred with the Japanese larch to form a breed which seems happy to be naturalized Scots.

Anyone wishing to look at woodland crossed by Picts more than fifteen hundred years ago should visit the shores of Loch Maree in Ross-shire. And in the peat bogs of Rannoch Moor, once the site of an Ice Age reservoir, there are also ancient remnants. In addition, fossilized trees may be seen at Victoria Park, Glasgow.

Clumps of fir trees abound by many lochs, and the Scots pine is still plentiful, providing food for a little bird called the crossbill, which eats its seeds. Sycamores and beeches are also common, and the sight of a beech wood in autumn with its fire-bronze leaves is memorable. Beech hedges are popular fences around large estates in the Lowlands. These estates may well have avenues lined with rhododendron bushes, which, despite the fact they were imported from the Himalayas, blossom abundantly in Scotland in hues of pink, red, magenta, and purple.

Scots definitely believe that "a garden is a lovesome thing, God wot," for the country is rich in all types—from the huge formal herbaceous or shrub gardens of large homes down to the pocket handkerchief patches behind small cottages. Plants grow abundantly, well watered by the rain, both in garden and hedgerow. Flying over Scotland is like flying over Ireland—the whole country seems like a vast green garden.

Since the Highlands are mountainous, alpine and sub-alpine in parts, the flora of the area are different from those in the Central Lowlands. Heather blooms in purple glory in the north and south, but the alpine zones of the Highlands have blaeberry, ling, and dwarf juniper along with alpine forget-me-nots and rock speedwell. And you'll find birds like snow bunting and the Arctic ptarmigan on the hill summits.

Experts say that the Highlands and Islands of Scotland remain one of the finest wildlife areas of the world, so if wildlife interests you, take the night train from London to Inverness and start exploring. Of the thousands of acres of national wildlife reserve land in Britain, more than 75 percent of it is in Scotland. And of that, much is in the Highlands and Islands.

The Highlands are the home of the fiercest animal in Britain, the wildcat, and of the rarest, the pine marten, which used to inhabit the ancient pine forests but which has now retreated from the paths of people and automobiles up into the mountainous areas. The only venomous snake in Britain is the adder, and there are some specimens wriggling around Scottish moors. The king of birds, the golden eagle, nests in summits like those above Invermark Forest and feasts on local mammals—rabbits, hare, voles, fieldmice, and young foxes. Other birds like the capercaillie (wild turkey), peregrine falcon, and kestrel, as well as more common ones like the blackbird, crow, and warbler, abound. The osprey, long feared almost extinct, is recovering and doing well in the Highlands.

Scotland even has a native equine—the Shetland pony from the islands of woolen fame. They are a small, shaggy breed and very popular with children all over the world.

One of the most interesting animals found in Scotland is the deer, which roams in the deer forests and corries of the Highlands and Islands. A deer "forest" does not necessarily mean that it has many trees—it may be largely high moorland. The roe deer are similar to the Scandinavian type, but the red deer is native. There are now as many red deer in the Highlands as there were a couple of hundred years ago —principally because the Red Deer (Scotland) Act of 1959 imposes closed seasons on both stags and hinds and levies penalties for infringement. Before the act was passed, there was a great deal of indiscriminate killing and maiming by poacher gangs who were not interested in preserving the species.

There are approximately one hundred and twenty-five thousand red deer, producing thirty thousand new calves annually. But the mortality rate of the calves is high, and only about 60 percent survive to adulthood. Deer society is a matriarchal one, with the older hinds in charge. Hinds bark when warning the herd of danger; the stags roar like bulls when in rut. When a fawn is born, its mother leaves it hidden in the heather or bracken for several days, return-

ing to feed it two or three times daily. She will not allow
the fawn to follow her until it is stronger. At first the calf,
like Bambi, is dappled, but within two to three months it
has lost its spots and becomes like the other adult deer.

Apart from human beings, the deer's greatest enemy, the
deer is plagued by tiny insects called midges. Midges are
very small flies (called gnats in England) which hang in the
air in swarms and love to bite warm-blooded creatures. People who visit the western Highlands and Islands in summer
are as aware of the midges as the deer but are more likely
to use insect repellent. The deer repel the midges in summer
by moving to higher ground—just as the reindeer of Lapland
migrate to high summer pasture.

By mid-September, the stags, who have been grazing
alone, are ready to lock antlers with competitors and get
together a harem. Then when the rutting period is over,
they shed their antlers, and lucky hill-trekkers sometimes
find a new trophy for their entrance hall.

Author Sir Walter Scott and artist Edwin Henry Landseer painted magnificent pictures of the Highland stag in
both words and pictures, and Victorians considered Highland scenes with stags or cattle a real addition to their
living rooms. The cattle in Landseer's paintings are a peculiar
type with long horns and shaggy hair, tawny brown in color.
These are Highland cattle. They look fierce, but in reality
they are peaceful beasts and stand around ruminating in
various fields and moors, allowing themselves to be photo-
graphed by tourists.

Fields and hedgerows in the Lowlands have plants and
flowers common to many other northern European countries—daisies, clover, vetch, hawthorn, wild roses, and
buttercups. Brambles are native blackberries that bear a
tart fruit in autumn. In the spring woods you'll find carpets
of bluebells, primroses, and wild anemones. The "bluebell
of Scotland" is like a tall, purple-blue wild onion flower

that grows in profusion in the glens. The little sweet-faced primroses have a delicate fragrance that the Scot abroad may remember for fifty years.

Common birds in rural areas are crows, blackbirds, song thrushes, robins, and sparrows, and in the fields you'll hear larks trilling. There are stinging nettles growing in clumps in ditches and glens, but the healing dock leaves always grow close by. If you ever get stung by a nettle, just pull a dock leaf, spit on it, and rub the sting hard with the leaf— the sore part will cool down immediately.

The moors have heather and rough grasses growing in tussocks, making walking tricky unless you have sturdy shoes or boots. The heather almost always blooms purple, but sometimes you may be lucky enough to find a white patch. In spring the farmers burn areas of the heather to encourage the growth. There are birds that live on the moorlands too— plovers, curlew, hawks and, of course, pheasant, partridges, and grouse for the hunters.

From the moorlands we turn to the coasts. The east coast has fishing villages and foggy summer mornings. The western Highland coastline has a unique belt of vegetation called in Gaelic the machair. The machair is a belt of natural grassland of mixed type that consolidates land first stabilized by the coarse marram grass. Marram grass grows by the sea on sandy shores and helps maintain a coastline which without its stabilizing force would be subject to rapid change. Below the machair, there are limpets, mussels, and sea urchins in tide pools and perhaps carragheen and dulse, which you can eat if you're so inclined. Processed seawrack makes good manure.

On the western side of some of the outer islands—Barra, the Uists, Tiree—you will find vast stretches of sand with nothing disturbing their smooth perfection save the tide and a few gulls. The famous white sands of Morar are of silica,

and there are coral sands on the Isle of Skye, by Loch
Carron, and near the Kyle of Lochalsh. Some of the Clyde
coast beaches are covered with large rounded pebbles, but
holidaymakers perch their deck chairs on the uneven ground
as soon as the temperature hits sixty-five degrees—that may
be summer.

There are great colonies of seabirds all around the coasts,
with oyster catchers common in the western Highlands. The
National Nature Reserves of Saint Kilda and North Rona
in the Outer Hebrides house some of the finest of the seabirds. Saint Kilda is the main breeding ground of the petrel,
and there are clouds of terns, puffin, and kittiwakes. The
little isle of Hirta holds the largest gannetry in the world.

The sea mammals found off the shore of Scotland are the
seal (the grey and the common seal), the porpoise, and the
sperm, blue, and killer whales. In sea-lochs the otter is
fairly common, sometimes coming quite far inland.

Many grey seals breed in Orkney and Shetland, and there
is a large colony of them in North Rona, where approximately twenty-five hundred calves are born every year. The
seals may travel far—from Orkney to Scandinavia or to
Iceland—during their lifetime.

Two kinds of sharks are found in the waters surrounding
Scotland—the small blue shark, which has become relatively
rare, and the basking shark of the Firth of Clyde and other
waters.

On land, Scotland's forests are being skillfully regenerated
with the help of the Forestry Commission, and there are
many forest parks, covering thousands of acres. Queen
Elizabeth Forest Park in the Trossachs area preserves land
once hard-traveled by Rob Roy and his marauding band.
Argyll National Forest Park, not far from Glasgow, provides
recreational facilities for weekend tourists from the big city.

But the Forestry Commission fights battles with weather,

small animals, and—a great enemy—bracken. Bracken is a tall, fernlike plant which has taken over half a million acres of grazing and growing land in the Highlands and turned it into wasteland. Its growth is the direct result of sheep farming, for sheep graze deep into ground cover, chewing it much more destructively than cattle, and making it almost impossible for new grasses to grow after a certain time period. The Forestry Commission has tried to combat the bracken by burning, flooding, and fencing, and by the thick planting of young conifers. Herbicides are also being used to control bracken, but cattle and new trees play the major role in the regeneration of spoiled land.

In 1965 the Earl of Dundee wrote a memo about the new Highland Development Bill, stating objectives and methods of improving the way of life in the Scottish Highlands. Of forestry he said, "If we make the mistake of giving too much land to forestry, the costs of our error to future generations will be negligible. If we make the opposite mistake of giving too little, we may lose the battle for Highland regeneration."

Certainly the Scots have no desire to hear a traveler say, as Dr. Samuel Johnson said in 1773, "From the bank of the Tweed to St. Andrews I had never seen a single tree. A tree might be a show in Scotland as a horse in Venice." So they are happy that their Forestry Commission is taking care of planting new trees by loch, field, and hillside, and keeping their country like the green garden they want it to be.

For further wildlife information, write:

Scottish Wildlife Trust
8 Dublin Street
Edinburgh EH13PP

The Nature Conservancy
12 Hope Terrace
Edinburgh EH92AR

A first-footer bringing the New Year and a traditional bit of whisky and coal to a Scottish home.

CHAPTER 14

HATCHES, MATCHES, AND DISPATCHES

WEDDINGS IN SCOTLAND usually involve eating on a large scale, and it would be a rare Scot indeed who would invite guests to partake of nothing but cake and punch.

For church weddings the banns, or notice of intention to marry, are read out in the churches of both bride and groom for several weeks in advance of the ceremony. During that period also, one or more parties may be given to honor the couple and perhaps special premises rented for some kind of "wingding." Like the showers given in the United States, some people in Scotland give what is called a spree, where gifts are given to help set up the new household. There may be dancing and games at the spree, and if you are to be chief bridesmaid (best maid), you will be expected to present the bride with a china teaset. Perhaps modern brides also accept plastic or pottery now too.

On the day of the wedding, certain traditions also apply. The bride's parents pay for the reception, but the groom pays for the flowers and the liquor, and the best man foots the bill for the minister and the taxis. Shrewd people, these Scots, sharing the cost. . .

The bride wears white and often has a sprig of white heather in her bouquet to bring her luck. The groom, if so inclined, may wear the kilt, and it is not unusual for his friends to form a special guard of honor for the couple as they come out of the church.

The wedding reception following entails a sit-down luncheon or dinner, and there are lots of toasts and speeches. The reading of telegrams from absent friends and relatives also plays an important part, and some traditional messages might be, "Good luck and may all your troubles be little ones," and "Lang may your lum reek" (meaning, may there always be a fire in your fireplace).

When alcohol is served, there is sometimes champagne but always whisky and often sherry too. The wedding cake is not the soft, spongy variety so popular in the United States, but always a rich, dark fruitcake with hard icing and a layer of marzipan. It is served in small pieces, and for friends who cannot attend, cake is put into small white boxes and mailed out. (If you receive a piece in the mail, put it under your pillow and you will dream of your future husband.) While the cake is being served, the bridesmaids distribute the favors. Those are the cake ornaments, like silver bells, flowers, silver horseshoes, and so forth. Traditionally the first favors go to the grandmothers, then the mothers, aunts, and so on until all are handed out. The top layer of the cake is always saved for the first christening.

In the old days in the Highlands a cake of shortbread was broken over the bride's head, and the pieces handed around. The girl who received the largest piece would be the next bride. (This was perhaps a substitute for throwing the bouquet if no bouquet was available.) Some weddings in remote areas went on for days, starting with a grand procession across the moors led by a piper who piped the participants into church, and continuing with feasting and dancing. There is still dancing at almost every wedding reception in Scotland.

The honeymoon is a fairly recent innovation. Country folk had no time for such luxuries. On the island of Barra, both mothers sprinkled holy water on the marriage bed to bless it, and on the following morning the bride would don a new bonnet called a curtch and begin her new life as a working matron.

With the arrival of babies came the christening. Most ministers today will not go to the home to christen the baby, as they often did in the past. Ceremonies are simple, but there is a custom which lingers on. People visiting a tiny baby for the first time will usually place a silver coin in its hand for luck. (It's up to the mother to remove the coin before it gets into the infant's mouth!)

When a death occurs in a family, arrangements are made for the funeral to follow within five to seven days. In rural areas the corpse is still laid out in the parlor and watched over by pairs of men. In Barra a plate of salt is placed upon the corpse's chest.

On the day of the funeral, food is served to guests, and attending relatives often bring some with them to help out. Women do not go to the burial. They remain at the home until the men return from the graveyard, although up until the nineteenth century professional female mourners were hired to "keen" (wail) behind the coffin.

Almost invariably after a funeral alcohol is served with the food. Often it is whisky and sherry.

It is common for families to buy plots in a certain cemetery, and it is especially important for many old Highlanders to be buried with their kin. It can be a punishment to bury them far away.

The funeral of a Highland chieftain or other notable is a great occasion to which hundreds will turn out. The coffin may be draped in the family tartan and a piper hired to play a lament for the dead. In an account of the funeral of the Duke of Sutherland in 1865, we read about seven thousand guests being provided with beef, bread, and beer after a procession one mile in length.

As a rule, however, the Scots are not mourners. The neglected appearance of many of their churchyards attests to that. Apparently they like to remember old friends as they were. Yet one of the most popular national festivals is Halloween, the night the dead are supposed to walk abroad.

The old name for Halloween was Samhain, and it was a pre-Christian festival. Instead of pumpkins, which do not grow in Scotland, the Scots use large rutabagas and call them turnip lanterns. Gangs of boys out on Halloween used to have contests to see who could snatch the most lanterns.

Children who go out on Halloween do not as a rule wear complicated costumes, but many of them blacken their faces with soot. They are called "guisers" (from the French "déguiser" to disguise) and go round knocking on doors and asking "Are you wanting any guisers?" If the householder says yes and opens the door, the guisers are supposed to earn their treat of candy, apples, or coins by singing a song or doing a dance or giving a recitation. If you don't open the door and you happen to live in a tenement house, the guisers may tie your doorknob to your neighbor's and run away sniggering. The original "guisards" of the Middle Ages used to perform mystery plays as they strolled from place to place. Today's versions are much less ambitious.

At Halloween parties children "dook" (bob) for apples and try to bite syrup-covered scones hanging on strings from a shelf or the kitchen pulley where clothing is aired. Girls who want to find out who their future husbands will be peel an apple without breaking the peel and then throw the skin over their shoulders and decipher the letter it spells. Others drop egg white into a glass of cold water by candlelight at midnight and read the picture—a custom not recommended for the queasy.

In an old-fashioned Halloween party game, the guests

would sit around the kitchen table with a large dish of mashed potatoes and spoons for everyone. The lights were put out, and everybody started to eat the potatoes in the dark, eagerly feeling for the trinkets hidden in them. A ring meant a wedding; a tiny china doll, a baby; a button, a bachelor forever; a miniature horseshoe, good luck. The same charms were often used in Christmas puddings.

Many ancient Halloween traditions have died out, such as putting crosses of rowan berries on gravestones to keep the dead from rising, hanging an animal skin on the front door to keep the devil away, and dropping a penny in the milk pail to stop the milk from curdling.

Similarly, other old festivals have disappeared completely. On Fastern's Eve (Shrove Tuesday) cock-fighting used to be popular, until it was abolished by law. On Saint Michael's Day, September 29, there used to be many processions in the Hebrides and special bannocks (oatmeal cakes) were made. On February 1, the festival of Saint Bride, fishermen on the island of Barra would draw lots for fishing grounds, for they believed that on that day Saint Bride put her hand into the sea to warm it.

On April 1, All Fools Day, Scottish children still shout "Hunt the gowk!" when they tease successfully, and on May Day there may still be some maidens who wash their faces in the morning dew to ensure beauty for the year, as their ancestors did centuries ago.

Although Christmas is now the year's greatest religious festival in Scotland as in many other countries, it was not always so. In fact, there are people living who remember working Christmas Day and getting two days off at New Year.

The week between Christmas and New Year is known as the Daft Days, with the daftest being Hogmanay, New Year's Eve itself. There are always dances, parties, and ceilidhs (Highland parties) on Hogmanay, and to some visitors it seems as if the average Scotsman feels a national obligation on that night to get "roarin' fu' " (drunk).

The chief activity on Hogmanay is first-footing. This is the custom of calling on your friends and neighbors after midnight to wish them a "Guid New Year."

The perfect first-footer, that is, the first guest to cross your threshold in the New Year, is male, dark-haired, and laden with food and drink. Red-haired people are considered unlucky, and all women fair or dark equally unlucky— although if they carry a small piece of coal, that's not so bad. As a first-footer you should always carry something good to eat like shortbread or blackbun and a bottle of something like whisky or wine or whatever you fancy. These will ensure food and drink at your host's house during the following year, and if you carry coal the house will also have fuel. No one must go out first-footing empty-handed.

In the old days in the Outer Hebrides boys went from house to house on Hogmanay, their leader wearing a sheep-skin on his back. When invited into a house the leader walked three times around the central fire, or in more recent times, clockwise around a chair, and invoked the Trinity.

New Year's merriment always includes the singing of Burns' song "Auld Lang Syne," which is traditionally sung by a group standing in a circle with hands linked.

The very words from "Auld Lang Syne," which means "old long since" or "the days of long ago," perhaps say more about the character of the Scots as a people than any other song. They love the past and still retain much of it in their festivals.

The piper honors a lowly sausage as the haggis is brought into the banquet hall on Robert Burns's birthday.

CHAPTER 15

CULINARY ACHIEVEMENTS

Be sure to heat the earthen pot
And have your water boiling hot.
Put in a teaspoonful per cup
That each of you intend to sup.
Allow to stand for minutes four,
Then off the leaves be sure to pour.
When serving put the milk in first,
Add sugar and allay your thirst.
With this delightful, fragrant brew
You'll be refreshed and live anew.

(—old recipe for making good tea)

YOU WON'T BE MORE THAN A few minutes inside a Scottish home before you are invited to have a cup of tea. No matter what the time of day, it's always teatime. In the Lowlands you'll be asked if you'd like "a fly cup"—a quick cup between meals. In the Highlands, if you cross a friend's threshold you may be invited to have "a wee strupach," which in Gaelic amounts to the same thing.

Tea has been the popular drink in Scotland for about two hundred years. However, it first had an unsuccessful introduction, when several notables pronounced it unhealthy and dangerous. But after that hesitant beginning tea made a tremendous thrust forward to become the national drink, even outstripping whiskey!

Scottish children are given tea from an early age and are

often weaned from the bottle to a milky tea mixture. Coffee is now catching up in popularity with the younger generation, but even if you have coffee for your "elevenses" in the morning, teatime in the afternoon remains a reliable constant. And if you're watching your waistline, beware the groaning teatable, because it's loaded with calories.

For afternoon tea, you may be served dainty sandwiches, homemade scones with butter and jam or honey, sponge cakes, drop scones, crumpets, biscuits (cookies over there are like biscuits here and vice versa), tarts, meringues—everything deliciously fattening. Most Scottish women are not as aware of figure perfection as their American counterparts. They certainly do not seem to feel guilty if they are overweight, because the teashops are always filled with buxom, cake-munching matrons.

Many Scottish women do a lot of baking at home and are usually good cooks. Since the climate is seldom very hot, a lot of soups and stews are prepared. Cock-a-leekie soup (chicken with leeks and pepper) is a popular national dish and, of course, Scotch broth has traveled far from Scotland. Real Scotch broth is made from a lamb bone, not beef, and has a unique flavor and texture since a great deal of barley goes into it—as well as many other vegetables.

There's an old story about Prince Albert, Queen Victoria's consort, who, having been impressed by the delicious Scotch broth made by Balmoral Castle's cook, went to the kitchen to ask her what was in it:

"Weel," the woman replied, "there's carrots intit and turnip intit and onions intit and cabbage intit and barley intit. . . "

"But what's 'intit'?" asked the Prince.

"Did I no' just tell ye, sir? There's carrots intit and turnips intit and onions intit. . .," and so forth.

Stews are usually of beef, sometimes of lamb, but that

has Irish connotations. The "roast beef of old England" is usually good Scots beef, and Scots share an enthusiasm with their neighbors for steak and kidney pie, the dish of stalwarts.

In the United States people eat an interesting (though revolting-sounding) substance called headcheese. The Scots' own particular version of jellied meat is known as potted haugh, made from beef shank meat cooked with knuckle-bones. This is later ground and spiced with Jamaica spices and then allowed to cool and set. Served with mashed potatoes, pickled beets, and rutabagas, it is delicious.

Different game birds form a substantial part of many rural Scots diets, along with rabbits and hare. Some natives eat venison from their hills and moors, but most of it is exported to Germany, where it is received with greater enthusiasm.

Scots sausages differ from American and Continental sausages in that they are not nearly so spicy and usually contain a certain amount of breadcrumbs. Better still are sausage rolls—bulk sausage meat formed into small rolls and baked in pastry coats. "Forfar bridies" are a local east coast version of this meat within pastry with onions added. These bridies are similar to English Cornish pasties, which were invented years ago by tin miners' wives, who wanted to send a compact, nutritious meal into the mines with their husbands. Forfar bridies, concocted by an enterprising baker, filled the same need for the coal miners.

Since Scots are very keen gardeners, they grow a lot of vegetables for home consumption—although the climate in winter tends to limit variety. The most commonly used vegetables are cabbages, onions, carrots, turnips (white and rutabaga, called "Swedes"), leeks, brussel sprouts, and, of course, potatoes. Most Scots still tend to feel that if you don't eat potatoes once a day you'll probably wither away and die.

But don't think they're completely provincial about all their food. On occasion they have even been in advance of their time. For example, Scotland used desserts well before England did, because of its close historical association with France. The French were the first to introduce puddings to the table as a separate course after dinner. The Scots followed suit and still serve a variety of delicacies to tickle the palate and stretch the willing waistline. A favorite is a hot sponge-cake steamed pudding. This kind of pudding is steamed in a bowl that has been lined with marmalade, jam, or lemon sauces.

The most famous of the steamed puddings is perhaps the "clootie dumplin,'" the Christmas pudding which is rich with fruit and Christmas cheer. Traditionally everyone in the family has a stir at the dumpling for Christmas, and trinkets are put in it for luck.

Since the whole of Britain had for years a very close association with India and many Scots lived part of their lives out there, curries have long filled a place in the Scots kitchen. This may seem rather strange when you consider the difference in climate, but occasionally the British had the good sense to adopt some of the customs of the countries in which they settled. Therefore, you'll always find curry powder in Scottish grocery stores, although you might have a long walk to locate a tin of chili powder or oregano. With curry comes chutney, and Scottish cooks make excellent apple and vegetable marrow chutneys which they often substitute for the imported mango variety.

Since nowhere in Scotland are you ever farther from the sea than sixty miles, it is a maritime country with a fondness for fish. The sea-lochs and waters of the North Sea and east Atlantic Ocean harbor some of the most delicious fish in the world. Few dinners are tastier than fresh herring dipped in dry oatmeal (steel cut oats), lightly fried in butter, and served with tiny new potatoes sprinkled with parsley. Herring for hundreds of years formed, along with oatmeal, the backbone of Scotland's diet. Fresh or salted or smoked, they were a staple both tasty and healthy, and if we are to go by the old saying that fish make brains, then the Scots can certainly attribute some of their ability to their fondness for seafood.

Local fisherfolk treat herring in different ways, so that in different parts of the country you might taste several versions. The herring of Loch Fyne well deserve the name of "Scotland's finest," and crates of fresh herring are still sold into homes all over the country. These are the silver darlings of literature. Kippers, which have often been slipped into old theatrical jokes, are herring split down the back and carefully smoked to give them a bronze appearance and a sharp, salty flavor. Kippers are a popular breakfast dish in Scotland, as indeed are many other fish. None of your Continental breakfasts over there! If the hotel says bed and breakfast, it means breakfast with something you can really start the day on.

You might begin breakfast with porridge or pease brose. (Don't ever ask for oatmeal, as that's the raw state only.) Porridge has been a national dish for hundreds of years. When most other crops failed, oats would always grow, and dried oats mixed with stream water had enough goodness in it to sustain life. So Scottish soldiers always went off to war with their bags of oats, which they either made up into flat cakes and baked on a griddle, or mixed with water to form a kind of gruel.

Pease brose is a different thing altogether and is little used any more. It is a fine bronze flour made from crushed yellow peas and is mixed with boiling water and served as a hot morning cereal with a spoonful of honey or golden syrup. (Full of vitamins and awfully good for constipation.)

It has a distinctive flavor, rather nutty and strong, and many attest to its great qualities.

After your hot cereal you may go on to bacon, sausage, and eggs or kippers or Finnan Haddie, followed by toast and marmalade or oatcakes—and, of course, cups and cups of hot strong tea. If you're very lucky, you'll get "baps" instead of toast. Those are big, soft, floury rolls that bring back memories of Sunday mornings spent with comic strips like "Oor Wullie" and "The Broons."

Arbroath, a fishing port on the east coast, is famous for its breakfast "smokies"—smoked haddocks prepared over oak or birch chips. Finnan Haddies, which take their name from the town of Findon in Aberdeenshire, are also haddock, but they are hung up a chimney to smoke over a peat fire. Fish of many different kinds—sole, halibut, hake, salmon, trout, plaice, flounder—are eaten all year round. And we cannot forget the unbeatable fish and chips, which is as popular in Scotland as it is in England.

"Awa' roon' tae the Tallys' and get twa suppers for the nicht"—which, being translated, means "Please go down to the Italian restaurant and buy two fish and chip suppers for tonight."

Fruits are not as available in Scottish shops all year round as in some other places. Some fruits like oranges, apples, and bananas are almost always for sale, but less popular fruits often have short seasons. Soft fruit grown in Scotland itself has a very short season, and once the four weeks of July have passed, don't expect to find many fresh strawberries. Raspberries and currants also have a brief life, but they're all appreciated in season and snapped up for jam-making.

No self-respecting Scots serve store-bought jam if they can help it. Popular jams are strawberry, raspberry, gooseberry, rhubarb and ginger, plum, blackcurrant, damson, and red currant jelly. The more exotic fruits like peaches, apricots, pineapples, and grapes must either be imported or grown under glass in hothouses, because Scottish sunshine is notoriously scarce.

Sweet things are very popular with Scots, who are not as aware of dental care as they should be. Candies are eaten by everybody and known as "sweeties." Nobody would think of going to the movies or the theater without a "poke," or a box of sweeties.

Seasonal foods like blackbun and shortbread are prepared every year by enthusiastic cooks. The main things to remember when making shortbread are to use butter and never margarine and to do the rolling on a cool surface. Blackbun is a rich dark fruitcake, black with little currants, baked inside a pastry shell. It is traditionally served at New Year and is often accompanied with a dram of whisky.

Perhaps the most "Scottish" food of all is the haggis, about which innumerable jokes have been told—the most popular one being that haggis is really a strange creature with horns which roams the Highland landscape.

The haggis is actually a type of large sausage. It is composed of ground ox liver and kidneys mixed with oatmeal and oxblood. This mixture is heavily seasoned and then stuffed into a sheep's stomach or paunch. Nowadays butchers are less picturesque and use sturdy plastic bags to make haggis—a word, incidentally, which doesn't seem to have a plural. People have thought of hagges, haggi or haggises, but haggis it remains for one or more.

Since many countries have a traditional food which involves stuffing meat into a skin, the Scots are not original with their haggis. But no other can boast a banquet at which the chief address of the evening is made to a sausage. Robert Burns's famous "Ode to a Haggis" is recited in hundreds of halls every January 25 (Rabbie's own birthday):

Fair fa' your honest sonsie face,
Great chieftain o' the puddin'-race!
Aboon them a' ye tak your place,
Painch, tripe, or thairm:
Weel are ye wordy o' a grace
As lang's my arm.

The haggis is carried into the banquet on a special platter, heralded by a piper, and after being placed on the table is "addressed" by a guest speaker. Some people are wary of eating this strange food, since it is greyish-brown in color, but many others find its spicy flavor delicious, and haggis has maintained its place on tables from Edinburgh to Edmonton, from Saint Andrews to Sidney—often in canned form, courtesy of Baxter Brothers. You may be able to buy it in the gourmet section of your local exclusive grocery store.

It is a sad thing that Scots cooking has not received a higher place in the hierarchy of world cuisine, for Scottish home-cooking at its best uses simple, nourishing foods and serves them in the tastiest of ways.

Fortunately many Scots hotel owners have come to realize that visitors want to sample the traditional food of the country and are now offering various dishes on their daily menus. The Scottish Tourist Board invites visitors to write for a leaflet entitled "A Taste of Scotland," which lists more than three hundred different inns and hotels in which Scottish food is prepared in the traditional manner.

Perhaps the following recipes will titillate your appetite.

SOUPS

At dinner [in Aberdeen] Dr. Johnson ate several plates of Scotch broth, with barley and peas in it, and seemed very fond of the dish. I said, 'You never ate it before?' Johnson, 'No, sir; but I don't care how soon I eat it again.'   (—Boswell)

One of the greatest trenchermen I ever knew was an old friend of my father, who had at one time been the heavyweight champion of Scotland—he was one of those heroes who tossed the caber as if it were a clothes pole and put the shot the way an average person would throw a bowling ball. He was a huge man whose girth in later years matched his height, and when he came to eat at our house, Mother was always glad of a well-stocked larder. His favorite dish was "Kale" as he called it—Scotch Broth—and this he considered my mother's specialty.

MOTHER'S SCOTCH BROTH

1½ pounds beef shank
1 small marrow bone
1 cup barley
1 cup small dried lima beans
1 parsnip
Small piece cabbage (¼ small cabbage, chopped)
1 small rutabaga
1 large carrot
2 leeks
1 cup peas (dried or fresh)
1 large onion
Parsley

Put the beef and bone into two quarts of boiling water and add barley, dried beans, and dried peas. Simmer for 1½ hours and then add the chopped fresh vegetables (except parsley). Cook for another hour. Half an hour before serving, add the parsley and fresh peas (if used instead of dried).

LEG OF LAMB BROTH

Use the ingredients above, but substitute the bone from Sunday's leg of lamb, and the broth will have a totally different flavor.

LENTIL AND RICE SOUP

3 ounces lentils (soaked overnight)
1 onion (peeled and chopped)
2 ounces rice
½ teaspoon curry powder
3 pints cold water
2 teaspoons sugar
2 teaspoons salt
1 teaspoon vinegar
1 tablespoon parsley
½ ounce butter (1 tablespoon)

Put water, lentils, onion, and curry powder into a large saucepan. Add one teaspoon each of the sugar and salt. Bring to a boil and simmer gently, covered, for about two hours. Add the rice and the rest of the sugar and salt, and simmer very gently for another hour. Before serving, stir in the vinegar and the parsley and add the butter. Do not let the soup boil after this or the butter will curdle. Serve at once.

TOMATO AND BACON SOUP

2 pounds tomatoes
2 ounces bacon
1 ounce shortening or butter (2 tablespoons)
1 carrot
Salt and pepper
1 medium onion
1 stalk celery
Rosemary
Parsley
1 quart of beef stock or canned consommé and water

Cut the bacon into small pieces and fry gently until lightly browned, using the butter if necessary. Cut up the vegetables small and brown them in the bacon drippings after bacon has been removed and drained. Slice the tomatoes and add them to the other vegetables; then add the stock and a sprinkling of rosemary. Cover and cook until tender. Rub through a sieve and return to pan; thicken with a little flour (making flour into paste before adding) and serve. Season with salt and pepper just before serving.

PARTAN BREE (Crab Soup)

2 cooked crabs
1 cup uncooked rice
½ pint cream
2 quarts chicken or fish stock
4 canned anchovies
Salt and pepper to taste

Pick all the meat from the crabs and set aside meat from the large claws. Cook the rice as usual, but add a little extra water so that it will be slightly soggy when cooked. Sieve the rice and crab meat (except meat from large claws) and stir until smooth, gradually adding the stock to pan. Add salt, pepper, and anchovies to taste. Heat gently but do not boil; add meat from large claws and stir in the cream immediately before serving. This is the best soup for tasting as you go along—cooks get all the fun.

MOTHER'S LENTIL SOUP

1 cup lentils
1 quart water
1 smoked ham hock
1 small turnip
1 carrot
1 small onion
Salt and black pepper

Wash the lentils and soak overnight. (If you don't remember to do this, and I often don't, just cook longer and keep testing.) Dice the vegetables and put them along with the ham hock and water into large saucepan. Boil and then simmer for two hours, stirring occasionally. Remove the hock and put the soup through a sieve. Reheat and serve with crisp toast, after seasoning the soup to taste.

SUPPER AND LUNCHEON DISHES

Whilst on Sunday the Presbyterian gentleman took a sparing refection of bread and an egg or cold beef between sermons, merely to allay the acute pangs of hunger, reserving his energies and carnal appetite for the supper; the Episcopalian after going to his meeting-house, had a substantial meal at midday, having no scruples. Hence it was a common saying that if you would live well on Sunday, you must take an Episcopalian dinner and a Presbyterian supper.

(Graham, *Social Life in Scotland in the 18th Century*)

KIPPERS WITH RICE BALLS

Imported kippers from Scotland and Canada are available in most American supermarkets—look for them in plastic pouches alongside the sour cream, herrings, and lox. If you have not already tried them, be a devil. They are a tasty breakfast dish and may also be served for a later meal with rice balls, which are a fine bland accompaniment. Steam or fry the kippers according to directions on the packet and serve with these:

RICE BALLS

½ cup uncooked rice
1 egg
1 small onion

2 cooked potatoes
¼ teaspoon dry mustard
Breadcrumbs
Shortening
Salt and pepper

Cook the rice as usual, and when it is ready, add beaten egg, chopped onion, and dash of salt and pepper. Mash the potatoes well with a fork, add the mustard to them, and add to the rice mixture. Shape into balls, dip in breadcrumbs, and fry in deep shortening until lightly browned. Drain well and serve with kippers.

SALMON — DISH OF KINGS

They say that the perfect way to prepare fresh salmon is to have a pot of salted water boiling over a peat fire by the side of the river or loch you are taking the fish out of. But since not many of us can do that, it may be prepared at home in the following way:

FRESH BOILED SALMON

Scale and clean a piece of salmon with as little handling as possible. Place in a deep pot and cover with cold water, adding a good sprinkling of salt. Bring the fish to a slow boil, skimming off the scum that will rise to the top. Cook the fish ten minutes for each pound. If it's less than five pounds in weight, cook it only eight minutes to the pound. Probe gently to test if done. Strain off the broth and serve hot with fennel and melted butter, or cold with sliced cucumber and lemon.

Or, in the manner recommended by Sir Walter Scott, "The most judicious gastronomes eat no other sauce than a spoonful of the water in which the salmon has been boiled, together with a little pepper and vinegar."

FORFAR BRIDIES

These tasty little pies were first made in Forfar, Scotland, about a hundred years ago by a local baker. They have been made all over Scotland ever since.

1 pound round steak
3 ounces finely ground beef suet
1 minced onion
1½ cups flour
Salt
Cold water for pastry

Cut the steak into narrow strips, then into one-inch lengths. Pound until the strips are thin and tender. Sprinkle with salt and pepper. Make pastry out of the flour with dash of salt and mix with cold water—only enough water to keep the flour together, a firm dough. Roll out thin and divide into three portions. Shape each portion roughly into an oval shape. Cover half of each oval with the meat pieces; sprinkle with a third of the suet and a little minced onion. Wet the edges of the pastry, fold over to make an envelope, and crimp the edges with finger and thumb. Make a small slit in the top of each bridie. Brush lightly with a little milk or egg yolk as desired. Bake in oven set at 400 degrees for about half an hour. This is a delightful supper dish.

HAGGIS

This Scottish national dish which Robert Burns revered is still made in Scotland. Although the recipe is not what one might call an everyday one, surely it must have a place in any collection of Scottish recipes.

1 cup oatmeal
1 beef liver
1 beef heart
½ pound minced beef suet

2 finely chopped onions
Salt
Black pepper
Water
One sturdy plastic bag which can be boiled (The old recipe
    calls for a sheep stomach bag—can you see the butcher's
    face?)

Toast the oatmeal in a very low oven until it is crisp. Wash
the liver and the heart and cover with water; bring to a boil
and simmer for two hours. Cut away all surplus gristle and
put through grinder with the suet and onions (the latter
may also be chopped instead). Season highly with salt and
freshly ground black pepper. Add a little of the water the
liver and heart were cooked in, enough to make the mixture
soft but still sticking well together when the oatmeal is added.
Stuff the mixture into the plastic bag, leaving it a little more
than half-full, because the mix will swell with cooking. Sew
up the end of the bag firmly and place in a large pan of hot
water. As soon as the bag begins to swell, prick all over with
a fine needle to prevent bursting. Boil slowly in this uncovered pan for about three hours. Serve very hot with creamed
potatoes and rutabagas.

STOVIES

The word *stovies* is a direct descendant from the French
word *étuver* (to stew) and is just one of many words
left from the Auld Alliance between Scotland and
France.

8 medium potatoes, peeled and cut up small
2 tablespoons roast beef dripping
3 large onions, peeled and sliced
Salt and pepper

Melt the dripping in a thick-bottomed pan and lightly brown

the onion slices. Add the potatoes and a cupful of water. Do not stir. Sprinkle salt and pepper on top. Simmer over a very low heat till the potatoes are tender—30 to 40 minutes. This is delicious served with second-day cold roast beef. I also serve it with cold tongue.

CLAPSHOT

This is a dish from the Orkney Islands, off Scotland's northernmost coast, an area originally settled by the Vikings. Many of the inhabitants still look as if they have just stepped out of a Norse saga.

6 large potatoes, peeled and cut up
2 medium rutabagas, peeled and cut up
Salt and pepper
Butter
Dash of nutmeg
Milk or cream

Boil the potatoes and rutabagas separately and drain well. Mash each of them and then mix them together, adding a generous amount of milk or cream and a large pat of butter. Season with salt and pepper and a dash of nutmeg. Yummy with haggis.

OTHER FAVORITES

PORRIDGE

The halesome parritch, chief o' Scotia's food. (—*Burns*)

The only true porridge is that made with fresh oatmeal. Quick-cooking cereal products are all very well, but no true Scot who values his kilt will accept them as a real substitute for porridge. I have used steel-cut oats to make porridge in the United States, but they really have to be well soaked beforehand to get them soft enough.

Here is the traditional recipe for making porridge the true Scots way:

Allow each person one cup of water, one handful of oatmeal, and a small saltspoon of salt. Fresh spring water should be used, and the best oats in the world come from the county of Midlothian.

Bring the water to a boil, and as soon as it reaches boiling point add the oatmeal steadily with the left hand while stirring briskly with the right. My mother always used a spurtle to stir her porridge (that is, a little wooden stick), but a wooden spoon is fine. When the porridge is boiling, pull it almost away from the heat but see that it continues to cook. Cover and cook for about 20 minutes. Add the salt after it has been cooking for at least 10 minutes, because it has a tendency to harden the meal.

Ladle straight into warm bowls and serve with individual pitchers of cream or milk on the side. Each spoon of porridge should be dipped into the cream on the way to the mouth. You may care to add brown sugar, honey, or syrup to the top of the porridge once it is on the plate. Some people I know like a knob of butter. A hot breakfast like that is guaranteed to "stick to your ribs" all morning.

HASTY PUDDIN' (A breakfast treat!)

Peel and thinly slice three medium onions and drop them into some melted butter in the frying pan. When they are golden brown, add two tablespoons uncooked oatmeal. Turn up the heat a little and stir the oatmeal well in among the onions. Sprinkle with salt and black pepper and serve with lots of hot buttered toast. Scrumptious.

BANNOCKS

There is an old Highland story that after the Battle of Culloden, when Bonnie Prince Charlie and the remainder of his army were fleeing from the field of battle, one of the people who helped them on their way was an old woman of the Mackintosh clan. Running away from the pursuing Redcoats, the soldiers had to cross Mackintosh country, and this old woman set up a kitchen by the side of the road to bake bannocks (oatcakes) for the fleeing Highlanders. Each man as he ran past picked up a hot bannock and went on his way. (Surely the earliest form of "running buffet"?) Of course, that old woman back in 1746 used fresh ground oatmeal and stream water and cooked the bannocks over a peat fire that lent them extra flavor. But we can still make good oatcakes or bannocks today.

6 tablespoons fine oatmeal (put the steel-cut oats through the grinder)
2 tablespoons flour
½ teaspoon salt
1 tablespoon melted butter or shortening
Boiling water to mix

Mix together the oatmeal, flour, and salt. Add melted shortening and enough boiling water to make a firm paste. Roll out very thinly and cut into triangles. Bake for thirty minutes in oven set at 325 degrees. Serve with butter.

TRIFLE

There are many ways to make a trifle, and this is only one of them. It's the one I happen to like particularly well.

1 large can sliced peaches
1 package raspberry-flavored gelatin
Yellow or sponge cake
2 tablespoons sherry

1 pint of custard
½ pint whipping cream
Raspberry jam
Grated chocolate to decorate

Put the peaches into a large, deep bowl (a glass salad bowl is good) and use their juice to help prepare the gelatin. (Use one cup of water and the rest of the juice for the liquid in gelatin.) Pour the gelatin on top of the peaches and allow to set. Prepare the custard—either use the packaged mix or make some yourself according to this quick method:

Add 1 tablespoon of sugar to 2 tablespoons cornstarch and mix to a paste with a little milk. Put into a pan and gradually add the remainder of a pint of milk, being careful to avoid lumps. Cook over medium heat, and when it is almost ready to boil, drop in two well-beaten eggs and stir quickly. Cook for another five minutes, making sure the custard comes to a boil. Allow to cool.

When the jello and peaches are set, cover with small pieces of yellow cake. Pour the sherry on top of the cake; then spread with raspberry jam. Pour the prepared custard on top of this and refrigerate again. Just before serving top with whipped cream and decorate with grated chocolate.

MARMALADE PUDDING

6 ounces white bread
3 cups milk
3 eggs
3 ounces sugar (3 tablespoons)
1 tablespoon marmalade
½ cup raisins

Grate the bread to make fine crumbs. Scald the milk and pour over the breadcrumbs in a casserole. Allow to cool.

Separate the yolks from the whites and beat the yolks with the sugar. Add marmalade and raisins to the eggs and sugar, and stir this mixture into the breadcrumbs and milk. Beat the whites of eggs until they are stiff, and fold them lightly into the pudding. Set the covered casserole inside a pan of boiling water and cook for about 1½ hours in an oven set at 300 degrees. Serve with hot custard sauce.

BROONIE (An oatmeal gingerbread from Orkney)

6 ounces oatmeal (1 cup)
6 ounces flour (1 cup)
2 ounces butter (¼ cup)
2 tablespoons molasses
1 egg, beaten
1 teaspoon ground ginger
¾ teaspoon baking soda
Buttermilk

Mix the flour and oatmeal in a bowl. Rub in the butter with the fingers. Add ginger and soda. Soften the molasses in a pan and add to mix along with the beaten egg and enough buttermilk to make the mixture soft enough to drop from a spoon. Put in well-greased pan. Bake in oven set at 325 degrees for about one hour. Broonie is done when it is firm in the middle.

OVEN SCONES

8 ounces flour (1½ cups)
1 level teaspoon cream of tartar
½ level teaspoon soda
1½ ounces butter (3 tablespoons)
1½ ounces sugar (1½ tablespoons)
¼ teaspoon salt
Sufficient milk to make a stiff dough

Mix the flour, sugar, soda, and cream of tartar together. Rub in the butter with the fingers and gradually add milk to make a stiff dough. Roll out on a floured board to about ½-inch thick. Cut into small rounds and place on greased and floured cookie sheet. Bake in oven set at 400 degrees for 15 to 20 minutes. Serve with butter and jelly or jam.

GRIDDLE SCONES

8 ounces flour (1½ cups)
½ teaspoon salt
½ level teaspoon baking soda
1 teaspoon cream of tartar
2 ounces butter (¼ cup)
Milk to mix

Mix the dry ingredients and rub in butter with the fingers. Mix to a softer dough than oven scones but not too soft for handling. Roll out on to floured board and cut into rounds about ¼-inch thick. Heat the griddle thoroughly and test by dropping a little flour on to it: when the flour browns slightly, the griddle is ready. Cook the scones on both sides, turning once only. These are delicious served hot with butter, jam, cheese, etc.

CLOOTIE DUMPLING

6 ounces flour
3 ounces shredded suet
3 ounces currants
1 ounce golden raisins
2 to 3 ounces sugar
1 teaspoon cinnamon
½ teaspoon bicarbonate of soda
Enough buttermilk or sour milk to make a soft batter
(about ¾ cup)

Combine ingredients. Dip a pudding cloth into boiling water (a flour sack dish towel is ideal). Place the center of the cloth in a bowl and draw the fullness of the cloth together evenly so that the batter is molded into a round shape. Tie it tightly with string, but leave enough room for the dumpling to swell.* Place a plate in the bottom of a pan and put the dumpling on top of it. Pour in enough boiling water to cover the dumpling. Simmer for two hours, adding boiling water as necessary. Turn the dumpling out carefully on a hot serving dish, dredge with fine sugar, and serve with a hot custard sauce.

* If preferred, pour the batter into a buttered mold to within an inch of the rim and cover tightly with buttered paper. Steam for about three hours.

The ancient highland fortress of Eilean Donan on Loch Duich.

CHAPTER 16

HOLIDAY RESORTS

SCOTLAND HAS MORE THAN the usual share of what out-
siders might call resorts—or places that are beautiful enough
to fall into that category. There are hundreds of small
towns and villages scattered across both Highlands and
Lowlands where tourists would be delighted to spend some
of their holiday time.

It is difficult to cover all areas, giving a fair chance to
each one and showing partiality toward none, and perhaps
this chapter will have omissions which another writer would
not have allowed. The places talked about here are drawn
from this writer's own preference or familiarity, but they
certainly contain some of Scotland's loveliest areas.

Starting from the top of the island, in Scotland's northernmost counties, you can find some of the loneliest country
in the United Kingdom. Most people know Caithness because one of the county towns, John o' Groats, is famous as
the most northerly town on the mainland of Britain. (And
thousands have traveled from Land's End in Cornwall at
the southwest tip of England to John o' Groats just to be
able to say they've seen Britain from stem to stern.) Thurso
and Wick are two of Caithness' fishing ports, one on either
side of John o' Groats. From there you may travel by sea
or air to the outer islands of Orkney or Shetland.

The next county south is Sutherland, infamous for the
Highland Clearances of the nineteenth century, but also

famous for its wild mountain scenery. There's good fishing in Lochs Naver and Shin, and the Dornoch Firth between Sutherland and Ross and Cromarty is bracing and beautiful. There is also a small thirteenth-century cathedral (which is still in use) to be visited in the town of Dornoch.

Ross and Cromarty, collectively known as Ross-shire, has a lovely coastline of fjord-like inlets stretching clear down to the Sound of Sleat, the slender channel between the mainland and the Isle of Skye. Ullapool and Gairloch are popular Ross-shire resorts (Ullapool has some interesting late eighteenth-century houses), and the small town of Lochcarron has graced thousands of Scottish calendars. Following the road south from Lochcarron you can visit the famous castle of Eilean Donan, an ancient fortress in the middle of Loch Duich, and another scene popular with calendar producers. Loch Maree, close to Gairloch, is one of Scotland's most beautiful lochs and familiar to many Scots since it is part of the Beinn Eighe National Nature Reserve. This is the country of the golden eagle, the wildcat, and the rare pine marten.

From the Kyle of Lochalsh in Ross-shire or from Mallaig in neighboring Inverness-shire, Skye is only a ferry-ride away. From Mallaig the journey is about five hours long, and the ferry stops at Armadale, Kyle of Lochalsh, Raasay, and, finally, Portree in Skye. For anyone who has ever wondered about the old Scots song, "The Road to the Isles" (just what is so great about the "far Cuillin" anyway?), go sailing up in the northwest and find out. You don't need your own boat. Caledonian MacBrayne runs ferry services all up and down the coast from the islands south to the Clyde and beyond. And if you haven't stood on the deck of a ferryboat, gripping the handrail and facing into that salty wind—try it.

Skye itself is the largest island of the Inner Hebrides and

is an artist's paradise of mountains, bays, beaches, and heather. The best time for the western isles is often the early summer or else September, when the weather is very mild. There are regular services for car and passengers to Skye and the other islands. From the northern towns of Ullapool, Kyle of Lochalsh, and Mallaig, there are ferries out to the outer islands of Lewis, Harris, and North Uist and to the smaller ones of Eigg, Muck, Rhum, and Canna. Farther south the town of Oban has boats leaving several days a week to the islands of Mull, Coll, Tiree, Colonsay, Barra, and South Uist. From Oban you can take the ferry to Iona, the original Christian center of Scotland, and you may also see Fingal's Cave on Staffa, immortalized by Mendelssohn.

Returning to Scotland's northeastern coastline, stretching eastward from Inverness, you will find a series of small towns. This is a great fishing area, and the towns' names have a quaint but practical ring to them—Nairn, Findhorn, Buckie, Portknockie, Portsoy, Banff, and Macduff. And how about Rosehearty? Nairn and Banff have excellent beaches for families with young children and, of course, there's always good golf.

If you're driving along this coast from Inverness, you'll want to continue as far as Fraserburgh and then swing south to Aberdeen to do some shopping. (Talking of shopping, and most tourists seem anxious to do so, the main shopping centers are Glasgow and Edinburgh. But Dundee and Aberdeen are also good shopping towns, and smaller places like Perth, Stirling, and Inverness have well-stocked stores too.)

From Aberdeen there are several routes you may choose. You may want to cut due westward along the valley of the River Dee, an area known as Deeside, and if the month is September and your dates are right, then you'll want to attend the Royal Highland Gathering at Braemar. Eight miles from Braemar is Balmoral Castle, Victoria and Albert's pièce de résistance, where the present queen and her family spend part of every year. If you cut south from Braemar you'll end up in the heart of Perthshire, but unless you take the road northwest a little way again, you'll miss some of that county's most spectacular scenery.

The best way is to take the A road north from Crathie to Tomintoul and from there to Grantown on Spey, which is a popular resort with native Scots. From there the road south goes through Grampian country. The Grampian Mountains have become a center for winter sports over the past twenty years, but even without snow they are majestically beautiful. And if you're lucky, you may see a stag silhouetted on the skyline.

At Carrbridge you may see and hear the story of ten thousand years in the Highlands, and the town of Aviemore is a tourist center where you can see some of the work of sculptor Henry Moore. Newtonmore, close by, was the first town to introduce the sport of pony-trekking, which has become so popular.

The road continuing south through Dalwhinnie and Blair Atholl passes through wooded country interspersed with shining lochs and rivers. Just north of Perth visitors should stop at Dunkeld to see the ancient cathedral.

Another route through the heart of Scotland is from Inverness south down the road following the Caledonian Canal which cuts the Highlands in two. The road may be followed farther from Fort William to Oban, where steamers are waiting to take you out to the islands.

The central part of Scotland, its waistland, is mainly composed of the counties of Stirling and Dumbarton, but to the east juts out the Kingdom of Fife shaped like a little Scottie dog. And to the west lie the scattered peninsulae of

Argyll and the southern islands—where the name of Campbell ruled supreme many years ago (and there are still a lot of Campbells around).

Fife is a county of contrasts. You can drive through dejected-looking coal-mining communities and an hour later be charmed by fishing villages like Crail, Anstruther, and Pittenweem. Or you can visit Saint Andrews, where golf was born, and walk along windswept sands fringed with sea grasses. University students brighten the town with their scarlet flannel gowns, and there are many ancient buildings telling part of Scotland's story.

The county town of Stirling is an excellent center from which to branch out in all directions on side trips. In the town itself the castle is worth a two-hour visit. It is the home of the Argyll and Sutherland Highlanders regiment, and they have an interesting regimental museum there. The panorama from the castle esplanade across the valley of the River Forth shows the Ochil Hills, the Campsie Fells, and the Lomond Hills encircling the meanderings of the Forth. The view to the north encompasses the Abbey Craig with the Wallace Monument and the pretty little town of Bridge of Allan. From the castle also the guide will point out the sites of six battles fought in Scotland's colorful past—Bannockburn, Cambuskenneth, Stirling Bridge, Sheriffmuir, and Falkirk (where two battles were fought).

The best way to see Stirling Castle is to walk up Saint Mary's Wynd, which has sixteenth-century houses in good repair. Argyll's Lodging and Mar's Wark lie just south of the castle, and the nearby Church of the Holy Rude was built in the fifteenth century and is still in use. Cambuskenneth Abbey lies below the castle on the edge of the river, and is the burial ground of a king and his queen.

From Stirling, Loch Lomond is only about twenty-five miles away. The road to it passes through quaint little towns like Kippen, Buchlyvie, and Drymen. Loch Lomond is Scotland's longest loch and one of the most picturesque. The "low road" may be the swifter, but the "high road" which passes the loch will give you glimpses of scenery you will long remember.

North of Stirling lies Rob Roy country—the Trossachs— where the redoubtable MacGregor and his band of free-booters roamed the hillsides and glens. Lock Katrine, Loch Achray, and Loch Venacher are the three Trossachs lochs, set like diamonds on a carpet of amethyst when the heather is in bloom.

Callander is a pretty town to stroll through, and if you are more energetic, Ben Ledi has a good path up to the top from which the view is superb. Aberfoyle offers pony-trekking and a marvelous view from the Duke's Pass, and there are tartans to gladden the heart of the tourist. Several miles to the north lie the villages of Strathyre and Lochearn-head. A summer evening spent in Strathyre is a restful experience, immortalized by the poet who wrote "the evenin' fa's gently in bonnie Strathyre."

Going west, you can drive to the seaside resorts of Dunoon, Innellan, Hunter's Quay, or Kirn because they lie on a peninsula of Argyll. But it's even more fun to take the car ferry from Gourock across the Clyde and feed the sea-gulls to the strains of "Sailin' up the Clyde, wi' a lassie by your side." You can take the boat farther and go beyond Dunoon to Rothesay and the Kyles of Bute. Anyone who has sailed around the Kyles on a fine summer day must remember how they looked like emerald velvet with the little stone white-washed houses clustered on the shores.

Rothesay Bay stirred the heart of one poet:

> It's a bonnie bay at morning
> And bonnier still at noon,

And bonniest when the sun sets
And red comes ower the moon.
When the mist is on the Cumbraes
And Arran's peaks are grey
The great black hills like sleeping kings
Lie round sweet Rothesay Bay.

The best-known town on Scotland's west coast is surely Prestwick, one of Britain's chief airports and its most fog-free (in spite of what they say about Scottish weather). Close by is the fair town of Ayr, celebrated by its son Rabbie Burns as the home of "honest men and bonnie lasses." Burns's cottage is open to the public, and the Auld Kirk at Alloway, where Tam o' Shanter watched the devil play bagpipes for a witches' dance, can also be visited.

The abbey country of south central Scotland is also known as the Scott Country, for Abbotsford, the stately home of writer Sir Walter Scott, is in the center. There's a twelfth-century Cistercian abbey at Melrose to visit, and at Mellerstain House you may see one of the finest Adam houses in the country. Sir Walter is buried at Dryburgh.

The most obvious resort town in Scotland to overseas tourists is the capital city of Edinburgh. It's the kind of place you go to when you want tickets for the theater or want to buy a new winter coat, and it's the place you take Aunt Nellie to visit when she comes home from Australia (or Canada or the United States) after twenty years. But it's not a resort to the Scots. It's certainly not where they would spend their two-week summer vacation. That vacation, or summer holiday, they're much more likely to spend at one of the spots mentioned earlier. They love the sea and the lochs and the countryside, and as soon as July comes to Scotland, they are on the move to hotels, holiday camps, caravans, and campsites.

Want to join the locals? They know where to go.

Alexander Graham Bell at twenty, three years before he left Edinburgh, his native city, for Canada and the United States.

CHAPTER 17

THE SCOTS ABROAD

> "The Scots transplanted from their own country are
> always a distinct and separate body from the people
> who receive them."   (—an old writer)

IF ALL THE PEOPLE claiming Scottish heritage all over the
world suddenly decided to move to Scotland, there would be
a national crisis. Some 20 million people in the United
States, Canada, New Zealand, Australia, and other places
can tell you today that their ancestors came from Scotland—
and what's more they often know more about their family
history than most of their relatives left in Scotland. Somehow
there's a strong tie that has bound them all to the old
country, maybe because it's made of tartan.

If you were to ask emigrating Scots today why they were
leaving Scotland, they'd probably tell you, "for better job
opportunities" or "for more money" or "to see the world."
Scots have been leaving home for the same reasons since
the sixteenth century and before.

Some of the earliest Scottish travelers were small-time
merchants who packed a bag of native skins and furs and
took themselves off to the Baltic States on independent sales
trips. They annoyed the English traders, who said they sold
too cheaply because the Scots could live on next to nothing.
More and more Scots took up peddling, and in fact the
word "Schott" became a synonym for "peddler" in the Baltic
States.

Historian Rosalind Mitchison says, "The great emigration of the seventeenth century is a commentary on the
failure of Scottish economy to expand as fast as the population." In other words, there were not enough jobs for the
boys so the boys took off to where there were jobs. Perhaps
as many as a hundred thousand Scots went to Sweden,
France, The Netherlands, Denmark, Germany, Poland, and
Russia, most of them enlisting in foreign armies. Scotsmen
had fought with Saint Joan, and the French kings had a
Garde Écossaise right up until the French Revolution in
1789. Gustavus Adolphus of Sweden had Scottish army
units, Frederick the Great of Prussia had many Scottish
friends, and a Scotsman, Samuel Greig, founded the Russian
navy.

When James VI went down to London as James I in
1603 to take over Elizabeth's throne, he took enough Scots
with him to start the local inhabitants wondering if there
would be any good jobs left for them. That may have been
the beginning of the tradition that Scots run things in
Britain (a belief that many Scots would like to foster) and
the foundation for this old joke: A Scot returning from a
trip south of the border was asked what he thought of the
English natives. He replied he hadn't seen any of the creatures, as he'd been only with "the heids o' departments."

James, however, did try to send some Scots overseas to
establish his new colony of Nova Scotia (New Scotland)
but found as usual that funds were scarce. At home James
was calling his new kingdom "*Great* Britain" anyway, despite
the facts that lots of his subjects were leaving for "furrin
parts." Many Scots indentured themselves as servants in
order to get out to the American colonies, and political
prisoners were usually sent there whether they wanted to
emigrate or not. Banishment was a common penalty in Scots
law courts of the seventeenth century, and the Americas

were lucky (or unlucky) enough to receive many sentenced this way. Many must have been unwilling—like the one mentioned in the account of the burgh of Stirling in 1699: An amount of rope is listed as having been purchased "to tye Laurance McLairen quhen sent to America."

One of the earliest and largest Scottish migrations was to Ulster, which was settled by perhaps as many as fifty thousand Scots in the early seventeenth century. This was James's way of trying to answer the "Irish question," which is still with us. This group in Ulster became known as the Scotch-Irish and was quite separate from other Scottish groups who later left Scotland for the United States. Many historians tend to confuse the Scotch-Irish with other groups, but much of their separate histories can be traced, and most of their development in the New World runs along different lines. Scottish Lowlanders, like the Scotch-Irish, however, never had the language problem that the Highland emigrants faced, and the Highland emigration from Scotland was a whole different fitba' game.

To begin with, the Highlanders spoke Gaelic, and most of them had little or no English. They tended to stick together after they left home, and once they had founded a colony, they didn't like to move again.

Why are there so many Macdonalds in the United States, and MacGregors, and Macnabs, and innumerable other Macs? Many were part of the great wave of people who left the Scottish Highlands between the early eighteenth and the late nineteenth centuries and came out to settle in a new land.

Early in the eighteenth century, before the Union of the Scottish and English Parliaments in 1707, a census tells us that England's population was six times as great as Scotland's, but England had thirty-five times the revenue and forty times the customs yield of Scotland. It follows then that many Scots must have been looking outside their borders for new homes, and Ian Charles Cargill Graham says, "By the 1770's the Highlander had come to look upon America as a veritable paradise of cheap land, low taxes, cheap provisions and high wages, where begging was unknown and the climate healthy."

In America there was "cheap land." In Scotland the land did not belong to the crofter, or small farmer. He rented it from the laird, or landowner, often through a middleman called a tacksman who had the power to evict when he saw fit. During the eighteenth century rents in Scotland shot up alarmingly, some as much as 300 percent in the Highlands. Taxes, or "rates," were also high. Food was never plentiful, and harvests were often poor because of abominable weather. When writers talk of "lifting the cattle" they mean it literally, for by spring the poor beasts who had had their blood let to make puddings in the winter had to be carried out to the spring fields. Wages were low, and begging not uncommon in both Highlands and Lowlands.

In 1770 a group of eight hundred people left Argyll (Campbell country) and wrote as reasons for leaving, "High Rents and Oppression" and "For Better Encouragement." The black winter of 1771-72 sent hundreds fleeing from the northwestern islands to the mainland for food. Snow had lain for eight weeks—an unheard of thing in those ocean-swept isles—and people and beasts were starving. Four thousand Macdonalds of Skye left for North Carolina in the four years after 1769 and formed a large nucleus at Cape Fear. Islanders from Uist and Barra exchanged their barren isles for Prince Edward Island. Between April and July of 1774 some five thousand emigrants left Scotland, most of them Highlanders who marched to the ports of departure in groups led by kilted pipers.

Newspapers sang the praises of lands overseas. In 1772

an Edinburgh paper advertised for settlers for Nova Scotia, promising "easy terms" which involved one hundred fifty acres of land to the first twenty volunteer families, with fifty acres for each child, relative, or servant at a mere seven cents per acre. The next twenty families were to receive the same but at fourteen cents per acre, and the next twenty at twenty-one cents per acre. Passages, payable in advance, cost eight dollars per passenger. No mention was made of the dense, uncut forest land of Nova Scotia, or of the climate, which was every bit as harsh as the Scottish one.

Ships of all kinds plied to and from the Firth of Clyde and the Americas, with Scots following after fathers and brothers, uncles and cousins. When Boswell and Dr. Samuel Johnson visited an emigrant ship in 1773 in Skye, Boswell looked on it with a kindly eye, pronounced it quite adequate as to accommodation, and contended that the dormitory-style sleeping arrangements were good, with each bed "fit to contain four people"!

An eighteenth-century man from the Hebrides wrote, "There were too many of us, which are reasons that some are come to seek their fortunes here."

And wherever they went, the Scots tended to do rather well. Not all of them were poor. Thousands of pounds sterling left Britain with the emigrants. But for the majority, poverty was their main reason for going, and when they reached the new land they set about establishing themselves with energy.

Douglas Young quotes from Sir Charles Dilke's book, *Greater Britain,* "In British settlements from Canada to Ceylon, from Dunedin to Bombay, for every Englishman that you meet who has worked himself up to wealth from small beginnings without external aid, you find ten Scotchmen."

The Highlanders joyfully wore their tartans (forbidden

in Scotland after the Jacobite Rebellions), wielded their weapons (likewise forbidden), and spoke their soft Gaelic as long as they could. The Lowlanders plied their trades and took up the business of merchandising with enthusiasm. They opened stores and took to importing and exporting and before long were running the tobacco trade. They even started chains of stores along some of the frontiers. Of course, many of them took up farming in the Americas' far more hospitable soil.

One successful store owner in South Carolina had done well enough in his new country to be able to leave an impressive list of worldly possessions on his death in 1751: glass decanters, drinking cups, plates, a teakettle, a spit, a chocolate pot, a coffee mill, three brass candlesticks, eight chairs, three tables, a bureau, a writing-desk, a couch and mattress, a featherbed, bolster and pillows, a hat and wig, a black coat and black plush breeches, a fustian coat and breeches, and a looking-glass. He also left behind two slaves, fourteen goats, and six sheep.

How did the Americans already well settled in the colonies feel about the Scots? Well, apparently they had mixed feelings. In 1739 a report from Georgia says, "It would be well for the Colony when the Scots and others that call themselves Gentlemen shall leave the Colony: for carrying over servants, they would not work themselves, nor employ their servants on their lands." And also, "It was very unfortunate for Savannah that the Scotch left their Country Lotts to live in the town, where they set an example of extravagance." (That's a new switch.)

The criticism about some Scots not being willing to work themselves undoubtedly stems from the fact that many of the tacksmen and lairds who emigrated hoped to continue the old feudal clan system in their new homes and clung to their old traditions as long as possible. The central factor of the tradition was that the laird was a patriarch to his people; they worked for him on demand, and fought for him, and he in turn looked after their welfare (as he saw it).

Yet many Scots earned independent places for themselves in the Americas. Thirty governors and lieutenant governors in the colonies during the eighteenth century were of Scottish birth, and there was at least one mayor, Dr. John Johnstone, of New York City. Dr. Adam Thomson from Edinburgh originated a new smallpox vaccination method in New York in 1755, and Dr. Peter Middleton, another Edinburgh man, performed the first human dissection in front of American students. Physicians and surgeons from Aberdeen, Dundee, and Perth all played important roles in colonial life, and two Scots, John Witherspoon and James Wilson, signed the Declaration of Independence. And what about John Paul Jones, founder of the U. S. Navy? He was originally from southwestern Scotland.

But, it's also true that these last three political figures were the exception rather than the rule at the time of the Revolution. As historian Graham says, "these few swallows did not make a summer." The Scots on the whole were a bunch of Tories, loyal to that same House of Hanover which had driven them out of their homes thirty years before after the Jacobite rebellion of 1745-46. Good old Flora Macdonald and her husband—that same girl who had rescued Bonnie Prince Charlie from under the noses of the redcoats —moved from the colonies to Canada because of her loyalist sympathies during the Revolutionary War.

"The loyalty of the Highlander in America to the Crown was a logical extension of his unquestioning obedience to his immediate landlord," Graham tell us. And since that landlord in America was often beholden to the Crown for the very lands he held, he was not about to jeopardize his position by joining any old revolution.

As the 1770s advanced, feelings against the Tory Scots ran high. One young officer of Fraser's Highlanders, having been taken off a ship and marched sixty miles, wrote about being cursed and spat upon as he passed through various townships.

Scots in Virginia had a bad reputation as moneylenders (shades of *The Merchant of Venice*), and in 1775 there was talk of "extirpating" them all together. Scots creditors were urging payment of debts before the war could cut off the possibility of collecting, and many Virginian planters were forced to sell their lands in order to meet their obligations.

Emigration from Scotland ceased abruptly with the start of the war—it was officially stopped in Britain—and people at home who had been concerned by the loss of skilled labor probably breathed a sigh of relief. Some of the colonies were equally pleased when it stopped, but not happy with what they were left with. In 1782 the Georgia House of Assembly issued an alarming document, an act whose preamble is as follows:

"The People of Scotland have in General Manifested a decided inimicality to the Civil Liberties of America and have contributed Principally to promote and Continue a Ruinous War, for the Purpose of Subjugating this and other Confederated States." The act then went on to forbid Scots from entering or settling in Georgia and promised imprisonment without bail to any who did so, with rapid deportation to follow. Exceptions were granted to "Scots who have exerted themselves in behalf of the freedom and Independence of the United States of America . . . and who are now entitled to the Rights of Citizenship in any."

But as with everything, time healed the gap between the immigrants and colonists. More and more people continued to leave Scotland and go to the new country, urged on by still another factor at home—the Highland Clearances. The major clearances occurred between 1782 and 1820 and again between 1840 and 1854.

Just how does one go about "clearing" the Highlands? A landowner merely evicts his tenants in favor of sheep. Sheep don't complain about the roof leaking and can feed themselves if the crops fail. Some lairds refused to do this, and there are stories of the gallant few who beggared themselves to support their starving tenants. But others turned men, women, and children out of their crofts and burned down whole villages. Donald McLeod, an eyewitness of the infamous Sutherland clearances, wrote, "the cries of the women and children—the roaring of the affrighted cattle, hunted by the dog of the shepherds amid the smoke and fire— altogether composed a scene that completely baffled description." The Macdonnells of Glengerry thrust out tenants who have never returned, and all over the Highlands lonely glens were filled with the bleating of sheep.

So the Scots continued to emigrate, and by the 1920s immigration to the United States reached its peak—more than three hundred thousand Lowland Scots moved to the United States looking for jobs. Some of them are still with us, and if you talk with them, you might think they had just left Glasgow the day before yesterday. More than 2 million Canadians today claim Scottish ancestry, and there are six thousand Gaelic speakers living in the Maritime provinces.

Scottish societies have sprung up all over the States, surely showing that the tartan tie still binds. The first Saint Andrew's Society was founded in Charleston in 1729, "to assist all People in Distress, of whatsoever Nation or Profession they may be," which was a remarkably progressive viewpoint for its day. The first Highland Games in the United States were held in New York in 1836. The first Burns Club was founded in New York in 1847, the first Order of Scottish Clans in Saint Louis in 1878, and the first Daughters of Scotia in 1898. There are now Scottish clubs in most large towns, and many places boast annual Highland gatherings.

Emigrant Scots and their descendants have made notable contributions to their adopted countries in government, the arts, business, and sheer adventure. Sir Robert Menzies was prime minister of Australia; Sir John Newlands, president of the Australian Senate; Peter Fraser, prime minister of New Zealand; and John A. MacDonald and Mackenzie King, prime ministers of Canada. Both Nellie Melba and Joan Sutherland whose exquisite voices thrilled millions of listeners, have Scottish origins. Andrew Carnegie from Dunfermline made a fortune in Pittsburgh steel and gave away four hundred million dollars to his town and old country. Alexander Graham Bell of Edinburgh invented the telephone and helped to found the Bell Telephone Company. John McLaren designed San Francisco's magnificent Golden Gate Park. And there were explorers all over the world who left Scotland for parts much more exotic—Gordon of South Africa, Mungo Park of Nigeria, Mackenzie and Fraser of Canada, Stuart of Australia, Moffat and Livingstone in Africa, Duff in Bengal, and many more.

Yet an old writer assures us that the Scots "have ever shewn the utmost aversion at leaving their country, or removing to happier regions, and more indulgent climes." And anyone talking with an exiled Scot today will have a hard time convincing him or her that there is any more beautiful country in all the world than Scotland—when the sun is shining.

APPENDIX A

ANNUAL EVENTS IN SCOTLAND

January   Lerwick, Shet-
         land Islands   —Up Helly A Celebrations
         Countrywide   —Robert Burns Birthday (January
                   25)   Curling, Soccer

February   Saint Andrews —Festival
         Glasgow   —Scottish Dairy Show
         Countrywide   —Soccer, Curling, Rugby Interna-
                   tional

March   Edinburgh   —Spring Flower Show
         Countrywide   —Soccer, Hockey, Lacrosse, Rugby
                   International

April   Pitlochry   —Opening of Drama Festival
         Edinburgh   —Opening of Royal Scottish
                   Academy Exhibition
         The Borders   —Rugby Sevens

May   Isle of Skye   —Skye Week
         Stirling   —Festival Fortnight
         Pitlochry   —Anglers' Fortnight
         Nairn   —Golf Week
         Cupar   —Agricultural Show
         Aberdeen   —Music Festival
         Countrywide   —Golf, Fishing, Pony-Trekking

June   Arran   —Welcome Week
         Melrose   —Festival
         Dunfermline   —Dunfermline Week
         Hawick and
         Selkirk   —Common Riding
         Linlithgow and
         Lockerbie   —Riding of the Marches
         Dumfriess   —Guid Neighbors Festival

	Galashiels	—Braw Lads Gathering
	Portree, Skye	—Skye Agricultural Show
	Oban	—Gaelic Mod
	Aberdeen and Forfar	—Highland Games
July	Annan	—Riding of the Marches
	Countrywide	—Golf, Fishing, Pony-trekking
	Airth	—Highland Games
	Balloch	—Highland Games
	Inverary	—Highland Games
	Stonehaven	—Highland Games
	Place varies with the year	—Scottish Sheep-dog Trials
August	Edinburgh	—Festival of Music, Drama and the Arts Film, Military Tattoo
	Invercauld	—Festival
	Dornoch	—Highland Games
	Mallaig	—Highland Games
	Strathallan	—Highland Games
	Ballater	—Highland Games
	Glenfinnan	—Highland Games
	Invergordon	—Highland Games
	Bonar Bridge	—Gala Week
	Dunoon	—Cowal Highland Gathering
	Countrywide	—Golf, Fishing, Horse Shows
September	Aboyne	—Highland Games
	Braemar	—Royal Highland Gathering
	Edinburgh	—Autumn Flower Show
	The Borders	—Sheep-dog Trials
October	Edinburgh	—National Gaelic Mod
	Place Varies	—Championship Dog Show
	The Borders	—Border Shepherds' Show
November	Glasgow	—Motor Show
December	Melrose	—Masons' Walk

Appendix B

PROVERBS

James Kelly (1721) says: "There are currently in society upwards of 3,000 proverbs exclusively Scottish. The Scots are wonderfully given to this way of speaking. . ."

A sillerless man gaes fast through the market.

They that deal wi' the deil get a dear pennyworth.

Dinna suppose that ye know a man till ye come tae divide a spoil wi' him.

It's over well hoarded that canna be found.

The man who goes once to Iona will go thrice.

It's ill wark takin' the breeks aff a Hielandman.

If ye hae little gear, ye hae less care.

The thing ye dinna ken doesna anger ye.

They who are early up and have no business have either an ill wife, an ill bed, or an ill conscience.

You will never grow howbackit [hunch-backed] bearing your friends.

Better a finger aff as aye waggin' [aching].

There's nane sae busy as him that has least to do.

Better speak boldly out than aye be grumplin'.

Two hands may do in one dish, but never in one purse.

Ill workers are aye gude onlookers.

The loudest bummler's no' the best bee.

He sits full still that has riven breeks [torn pants].

Appendix C

SAYINGS AND RHYMES

It taks' a lang spoon tae sup wi' the devil—or wi' a Fifer.

Cheese—moose's beef.

He's awa' wi' the fairies [he's daft.].

Don't lose your wig.

That's the ba' on the slates now.

Haud yer wheesht.

A sweetie wife [a gossip].

Blaw yer pipes and beat yer drum,
The best o' life is yet to come.

He thinks he's big but a wee coat fits him.

A wee toe-rag [a wild child, from *tuareg* an Arabic word].

To go a message [to run an errand].

Wait till you get hame and you'll get your lumps [you'll get spanked].

Awa' and raffle yersel.

I'll put your gas on a peep.

She's got her feet well under the table.

Mockin's catchin'.

Who stole your scone?

How can ye dae ocht when ye've nocht tae dae ocht wi'?

As fu' as a whelk.

The wind's high, it'll soon be rainin'.

Christopher Columbus was a great man,
Went to America in an old tin can.

What a fankle [mess].

Bide a wee.

The games a bogie, the man's in the lobby!

> Murder, murder, polis
> Three stair up
> The woman in the middle door
> Hit me wi' a cup
> Ma nose is a' bleedin'
> And ma face is a' cut
> Murder, murder, polis
> Three stair up.

> O, ma mammy killed me
> Ma daddy ate ma bones
> Ma two wee sisters buried me
> Between twa marble stones.

> Mammy made a dumpling
> She made it awful nice
> She cut it up in slices
> And gave us a' a bite.
> Tak' it, tak' it, don't say no
> For tomorrow is my wedding day
> And I must go.

> P.K. penny packet
> First you chew it, then you crack it
> Then you stick it to your jacket
> P.K. penny packet.

> Dance tae yer Daddy, ma bonnie wee laddie
> Dance tae yer Daddy, ma bonnie wee lamb
> You shall get a fishie on a little dishie
> You shall get a herring when the boat comes hame.

> See the little sandy girl sittin' on a stane
> Cryin' weepin' all the day alane
> Rise up, sandy girl, wipe your tears awa'
> Choose the one you love the best and tak' him awa'.

Ye canny push yer Granny off a bus
Ye canny push yer Granny off a bus
No, ye canny push yer Granny, for she's yer Mammy's
    Mammy
No, ye canny push yer Granny off a bus.

Annie Rooney had a wean
Someone hit it wi' a stane
The polis said it was a shame
Because it was a nice wee wean.

APPENDIX D

EMBLEM, FLAGS, AND MOTTO

The purple thistle, which botanists say is not even native to Scotland, is the emblem of Scotland. Legend has it that an invading Dane, one of a band who had come ashore to pillage, stepped on a bed of thistles and cried out loud in pain. This warned the native Gaels, who were able to ward off their enemy.

There are two flags commonly flown in Scotland: one the blue and white cross of Saint Andrew, and the other the scarlet and gold rampant lion. The cross of Saint Andrew is a white diagonal cross on a blue ground, and Andrew is the country's patron saint.

Scotland's motto is, "Nemo me impune lacessit"—No one provokes me with impunity—or None daur meddle wi' me!

APPENDIX E

SCOTTISH ORGANIZATIONS

Academy of Piping
127 Rose Street Lane South
Edinburgh EH2 4BB

An Comunn Gaidhealach
Abertarff House
Inverness IV1 1EU

Association of Gaelic Choirs
J. C. Sinclair
29 Slamannan Road
Falkirk

Burns Federation
Dick Institute
Elmbank Avenue
Kilmarnock KA1 3BU

Celtic Union
J. F. Hughson
16 Willowbrae Road
Edinburgh

College of Piping
20 Otago Street
Glasgow W.2

Films of Scotland
Film House
3 Randolph Crescent
Edinburgh EH3 7TH

Highlands and Islands
    Development Board
Bridge House
27 Bank Street
Inverness IV1 1QR

Royal Caledonian Curling
    Club
2 Coates Crescent
Edinburgh EH3 7AL

Royal Scottish Country Dance
    Society
Hdqtrs., 12 Coates Crescent
Edinburgh EH3 7AF

Royal Scottish Pipers' Society
25 Craigleith View
Edinburgh EH4 3JZ

St. Andrew Society
24 Hill Street
Edinburgh EH2 3JZ

Saltire Society
Gladstone's Land
483 Lawnmarket
Edinburgh EH1 2NT

Scots Ancestry Research
    Society
20 York Place
Edinburgh EH1 3EP

Scottish Civic Trust
24 George Square
Glasgow G2 1EF

Scottish Film Council
16-17 Woodside Terrace
Glasgow G3 7XN

Highland Pipers' Society
D. Cameron
12 Brunstane Drive
Edinburgh EH16 2NF

National Trust for Scotland
5 Charlotte Square
Edinburgh EH2 4DU

Scottish Pipe Band Assoc.
Headquarters & College
45 Washington Street
Glasgow W.2

Scottish Tartans Society
Broughty Castle Museum
Broughty Ferry, Dundee
DD5 2BE

Scottish Tourist Board
Ravelston Terrace
Edinburgh 4

ACKNOWLEDGMENTS

I would like to thank the following people and organizations for their assistance:

John M. MacGregor, La Jolla, California
Duncan Lewis Mackenzie Macfarlane, Guildford, England
Hamish and Wilma Robertson, Stirling, Scotland
David and Margaret Middleton, Dundee, Scotland
John and Helen Christie, Pacific Palisades, California
Commander Peter Cockburn-Thorpe, Fallbrook, California
Frank Searle, Loch Ness, Scotland
Mary Walling, Sierra Madre, California
I.S.G. Carmichael, Method Publishing Co., Sutherland, Scotland
Messrs. Ballantyne of Peebles
Messrs. MacDougall of Lanark
Scotch Whisky Association
Scottish Tourist Board
British Tourist Authority
National Trust for Scotland
Glasgow Parks & Botanic Gardens
David Patton, Scottish National Party
Patricia Beatty
Hazel Bain
Nan Wotherspoon
Perth Repertory Theatre — Mr. Andrew McKinnon
Dundee Rep. Theatre — Mr. David McNally
Traverse Theatre Club — Mr. John Carnegie, Edinburgh

Byre Theatre — Mr. A. B. Paterson, Saint Andrews
Royal Lyceum Theatre Company — Mr. Clive Perry,
    Edinburgh
Citizens Theatre — Mr. Giles Havergal, Glasgow
Mull Little Theatre — Barrie and Marianne Hesketh
Helen Jones and her writing group, Altadena, California
The Lunch Bunch, San Marino Library, California
The Blue Monday Writers, Pasadena, California

I also wish to acknowledge all the help and encouragement given to me indirectly in the past by teachers who first made me aware of Scotland's heritage. These were Miss Jessie Thomson of Stirling High School and Professor Mackie and Dr. George Pryde of Glasgow University.

The photos are reproduced through the courtesy of the British Tourist Authority, the Scottish National Portrait Gallery, and the American Telephone and Telegraph Company.

SELECTED BIBLIOGRAPHY

Bingham, Madeleine. *Scotland under Mary Stuart.* New York: St. Martins Press, 1973.

Burnett, W. B. *Scotland Laughing.* Edinburgh: Albyn Press, 1955.

Cowie, Donald. *Scotland, Land and People.* Cranbury, New Jersey: A. S. Barnes, 1973.

Darling, F. Fraser, and Boyd, J. Morton. *The Highlands and Islands.* Glasgow: Collins, 1970.

Dickinson, W. Croft and Pryde, George S. *A New History of Scotland.* London: Nelson, 1961.

Dinsdale, Tim. *Project Water Horse.* London: Routledge & Kegan Paul, 1975.

————. *Loch Ness Monster.* London: Routledge & Kegan Paul, 1961.

Grant, I. *Highland Folkways.* London: Routledge & Kegan Paul, 1961.

Harrison, E. S. *Scottish Woollens.* Edinburgh: National Association of Scottish Woollen Manufacturers, 1956.

Hides, Margaret. *Scotland.* New York: Scribner's, 1973.

Kermack, W. R. *The Scottish Highlands.* Edinburgh: W. & A. K. Johnston, 1957.

McIntosh, I. G. and Marshall, C. B. *The Face of Scotland.* New York: Pergamon, 1966.

Mackenzie, Alexander. *The Prophecies of the Brahan Seer.* Golspie, Scotland: Sutherland Press, 1970.

Maclean, Alistair. *Alistair Maclean Introduces Scotland.* Edited by Alastair Dunnett. New York: McGraw Hill, 1972.

Mitchison, Rosalind. *A History of Scotland.* London: Methven, 1970.

Moncreiffe, Iain. *The Highland Clans.* New York: Potter, 1968.

Reid, James M. *Scotland's Progress.* London: Eyre, 1971.

Smith, Adam. *Life among the Scots.* New York: McGraw Hill, 1966.

Thomson, Jessie, and Strachan, Robert. *From Castle Rock to Torbrex.* Edinburgh: Cunningham and Sons, 1962.

Thornhill, Martin. *Explorer's Scotland.* New York: Roy, 1953.

INDEX